LEADERSHIP
BEEF
JERKY

Principles and Practices You Can Chew On

——

DR. GREGORY W. BOURGOND

LEADERSHIP BEEF JERKY
PRINCIPLES AND PRACTICES YOU CAN CHEW ON

THE HOLY BIBLE, NEW INTERNATIONAL VERSION®, NIV® Copyright © 1973, 1978, 1984, 2011 by Biblica, Inc.® Used by permission. All rights reserved worldwide.

iUniverse books may be ordered through booksellers or by contacting:

iUniverse
1663 Liberty Drive
Bloomington, IN 47403
www.iuniverse.com
844-349-9409

ISBN: 978-1-5320-4719-0 (sc)
ISBN: 978-1-5320-4718-3 (hc)
ISBN: 978-1-5320-4720-6 (e)

Library of Congress Control Number: 2018904467

Print information available on the last page.

iUniverse rev. date: 12/01/2021

And what you have heard from me in the presence of many witnesses
entrust to faithful men who will be able to teach others also.
—2 Timothy 2:2

To my grandchildren, Derrick, Braedan, Talisa, Kieran, Gaelan,
and Lochlan, I dedicate this book. May the lessons contained
within serve as a compass for the road ahead as you each take
your place of leadership within your sphere of influence.
—*Papa*

CONTENTS

HAND

FOREWORD

Just as Rome wasn't built in a day, wisdom isn't attained in a day. It's always the by-product of a lifetime of study, reflection … and action.

It's been my rare privilege to know Greg Bourgond over the long stretch of more than forty years. I say "rare" because the truth is, it's not often that we find someone who significantly shares our DNA. Greg and I have served in church together, mentored countless men, and tried our best to develop our leadership chops—*not for self-aggrandizement* but with the goal of building God's kingdom. And we have been the beneficiaries of an incredible journey of friendship all along the way.

The late Bill Bright, founder of Campus Crusade for Christ (now CRU), was a man I deeply admired. His passion for people, for sharing the love of Jesus, and for identifying the potential in others has long served as a model. I had the privilege of being on stage at a Promise Keepers men's rally in Orlando, Florida, years ago, when many of us gathered around him to seek God's blessing on his eightieth birthday. At the time, he was already ailing from the disease that would eventually take his life.

The fascinating thing about Dr. Bright is that when he discovered he had a debilitating disease that would lead to his death, he doubled down on life. Rather than give up, he upped the ante. He did everything he could to take the lessons learned over a lifetime and pass them on to the next generation of leaders. But what impressed me most was his passion to "give back" everything God and others had poured into him. In his own unforgettable words, he wanted to "die empty."

I want to die like that, and I know that Greg feels the same way. It's in the nature of warriors to want to leave it all on the battlefield. Having said that, the cause truly matters. Warriors aren't willing to die for just any old cause. As you will soon discover in this primer on leadership, wise leaders carefully discern which hills are worth dying on and which ones aren't.

Greg has done us all a great service by his willingness to "die empty." This volume represents the distillation of leadership lessons and principles won at great personal cost over the years.

In closing, I would be remiss if I failed to say a couple of more things about my best friend. Greg never pursues anything half-heartedly. It's why I've always been quick to listen to (or read) anything he has to say. You can be confident that not a single word that appears in the following passages is accidental or incidental. The topics he "speaks into" are ones he has faced and wrestled with and are thus completely devoid of pie-in-the-sky, ivory-tower thinking.

The other thing I would say about Greg is that he is a genuine lover of Jesus. I don't say that lightly in an era when so many once-fine leaders have defected from the faith. Following hard after him carries a steep price tag. That's because Christianity always has—and always will be—countercultural at its core. It's in that spirit that I heartily commend this volume to you.

If a friend can also be a hero, I am twice blessed.

Dr. Gary Gonzales
Redmond, Washington

ACKNOWLEDGMENTS

J. Robert Clinton

Bobby, as he prefers to be called, is my mentor. From him I have learned what it means to be a biblical-centered leader. He has taught me that godly character informs what we do. I am indebted to him for understanding how leaders are developed. The reader will see his fingerprints throughout this book. His blessing of me gave me the direction I needed to make sure I finished well.

Erwin McManus

Erwin sees me for who I am and what I can contribute to facilitate God's redemptive purposes. He is a friend and adviser who isn't afraid to hold me accountable to my calling. He has mentored me in person and from a distance through his messages and books. He challenges me to never be satisfied with being average. His life story inspires me to be all God intended to be.

Jerry Sheveland

I have learned a great deal about leadership from Jerry. I have watched him lead through example. As his executive pastor, he showed me how to bring a vision alive and mobilize others around a vision. His wise counsel has informed tough decisions I have made. His unflagging support encouraged me to find my unique voice. He has set the bar for godly leadership and the exercise of integrity in the face of opposition.

Leland Eliason

Leland saw more in me than I did in myself. He gave context to my leadership and sponsored me as I grew in responsibilities. He gave me opportunities to fly. His candid evaluations compelled me to strive for excellence. He didn't pull punches when I needed to correct my leadership going forward. I wouldn't be the leader I am today without his influence in my life. I will be forever grateful for what he taught me.

Gary Gonzales

Gary has been my best friend for over four decades. I asked him to write the foreword of this book because he knows me best. God has placed Gary at the juncture of every critical event in my life. I can count on him to give me solid counsel and wise direction. He has never failed to advocate for me when it matters. He is a model of integrity, honor, and authenticity. He is in my corner, always encouraging me forward.

Debby Bourgond

My wife gives me the platform I get to dance on. Her unfailing love, encouragement, and support inspired me to accomplishments I wouldn't have attained otherwise. She is my greatest ally. She sees me in the light and in the dark and loves me regardless. She is a model of loving nurture who is the mortar that holds the bricks of my leadership together. I cannot imagine life and ministry without her advice and guidance.

INTRODUCTION

The question you might be asking is, "Do we really need another book on leadership?" A simple search of leadership books on Amazon yields over 192,000 results. Yet books on leadership find a ready market for men and women looking for the principles and practices that will help them become better and more effective leaders. Whether we want to admit it or not, we seek the holy grail, the silver bullet that will unlock the mystery of becoming a great leader. I would like to add my contribution to your ongoing development, whether you are a reluctant leader, a polished leader, or you don't think you are a leader at all. I remind you that any time you make a decision that will affect others, you are leading, whether in the home or the marketplace.

When someone looks at my resume, they may conclude there is no rhyme or reason to it. An intentional pattern is not discernible. Yet, in retrospect, I see God's fingerprints throughout. We are the sum of our experiences, the products of our opportunities, the reflections of our circumstances, and the beneficiaries of guidance from our relational and professional guides. We have benefitted from nonformal, informal, and formal training and education. We have learned, over time, what works and what doesn't work. Hopefully, we have learned from our mistakes and failures, our disappointments and discouragements, and our successes and triumphs.

My experience is eclectic. In addition to entry-level jobs, I have worked for a manufacturing company as a plant engineering draftsman, a navy chief in antisubmarine warfare, a lieutenant commander in naval intelligence, a principle analyst for a defense company, a project engineer for a major aerospace and defense contractor, an operations engineer and training unit manager for a leading undersea systems company, a general manager for an automobile dealership, a pastoral staff coordinator and adult ministries pastor for a megachurch, a dean of academic affairs and instructional technology, a director of doctoral programs, a vice president of operations and strategic initiatives for a graduate theological school, a director of strategy for online education at a university, an executive pastor for a large church, founder and president of a men's ministry organization, and an adjunct professor for two graduate schools.

In nearly seven decades, I have had opportunity to serve in a variety of circumstances, including the military, commercial business, the defense industry, higher education, and ministry. I believe I know what works and what doesn't work. I have had the benefit of many mentors and platforms to exercise leadership. I have witnessed firsthand the efficacy of certain principles and practices.

Ten foundational principles have underpinned my practice of leadership and conditioned how I lead.

1. Mission: Fulfilling the great commission (Matthew 28:19–20) in our communities requires transformed churches led by transformed leaders who are obedient to the great command (Matthew 22:27–37).
2. Training: God is building an army of transformed leaders for the new millennium. Christian leaders will stand out in bold relief against the backdrop of their culture. We are now being trained for such a time in the "in-between time."
3. Character: Effective godly leadership flows from "being," is a matter of the heart, and is character-centered, not skill-centered. Skills are the tools of effective leadership; character is the power of effective leadership.
4. Battlefield: Lasting behavioral change that brings glory to God begins with the heart, in general, and our core belief system. Satan's battlefield has never been our behavior; it has always been the heart.

5. Purpose: The ultimate purpose of the church is to produce Christlikeness in its followers, beginning with salvation, continuing with sanctification, and concluding with glorification.
6. Authenticity: Authentic spirituality is a prerequisite for godly leadership and is produced when we tune our lives to God's standards of excellence. Its vitality comes from living our lives for an audience of One.
7. Effectiveness: Effective godly leadership is developed over a lifetime, is exercised through our God-given passion and giftedness, finds its source and authority in God, is built on biblical principles and values, and is practiced in culturally sensitive ways.
8. Credibility: The distance out front a leader is permitted to lead is directly proportional to the credibility that leader has with those being led. Willing followership depends on the status of our bank accounts of credibility.
9. Personal: Effective leaders know the capabilities, limitations, weaknesses, and potential of their followers. The leader is responsible for providing opportunities for people to realize their potentials in Christ.
10. Servanthood: Effective godly leadership is servant leadership. Servant leadership manifests spiritual authority and is credible when the leader is what he/she teaches. It comes from a life and a ministry that demonstrates the presence of God and understands the purposes of God.

I have had roles as a teacher and professor, analyst, engineer, manager in multiple capacities, executive leader of organizations, military enlisted and officer, president and founder, consultant, mentor, and writer. I have led small and large groups of employees in numerous settings and situations. During my life, I have been exposed to myriad leadership principles and practices, effective and ineffective, faddish and timeless, and productive and nonproductive.

I personally have observed or implemented leadership principles and practices that have withstood the test of time and have proven to be transformative, transferable, and transitional. These principles and practices could be categorized under leadership congruence, leadership character, or leadership competence—the three primary arenas of leadership development.

Books on leadership competence abound because it is the easiest area to address. Who doesn't want better competencies, skills, methodologies, tactics, strategies, procedures, or a new approach? However, who you are as a leader—your character and how your wiring plays a role in your practice of leadership—your congruence, will determine how effective your implementation of leadership practices will be.

The title of this book, *Leadership Beef Jerky*, is more than an attention-grabber. Beef jerky, it seems, lasts forever. It retains its nourishment over time. But to enjoy its benefits it must be chewed one chunk at a time. It is healthy, convenient, and portable. To get the most from this book, readers can move about the chapters and find what is applicable for their needs now. The book is not meant to be read from beginning to end but more like a smorgasbord, where you go along the line and pick what you want or need at the stage of your life.

For a simpler arrangement, I have divided principles and practices under three categories: *Head*, *Heart*, and *Hand*. What we know, what will inform our leadership, and what activities will help us lead more effectively address the three primary spheres of influence we will wield. Chapters under these headings are not exhaustive but succinct. They are not written to cover each topic completely but to focus on what is essential to be, to know, and to do.

Under "Head," you will find principles and practices that help organize how you think about leadership and what will and should inform your understanding and practice. Deciding the big questions about beingness will enlighten our practice of doingness. In this section, you will find helpful information to calibrate your thinking about leadership practice.

- Where and when to engage (prioritizing)
- Providing margin for growth, creativity, and innovation (margin)

- Making good decisions (discerning)
- Filling your mind with God's mind (meditating)
- Grasping reality and adjusting expectations accordingly (perceiving)
- Understanding boundary events that move us to the next thing (transitioning)
- Avoiding barriers and finishing well (finishing)
- Absorbing what matters using the reading continuum (reading)

Under "Heart," you will be introduced to calibration of the soul. We are told to guard our hearts because it will bring forth, good or bad, what is stored within.[1] Out of the heart flows the wellspring of our lives. Calibration of the heart to the heart of God is essential to accomplish God's redemptive purposes in the world. In this section, you will be introduced to the following topics that will attune your heart for leadership practice:

- Determining your destiny (calling)
- Identifying the principles you will live by (values)
- Living a life of congruity (integrity)
- Finding direction for your life (compass)
- The importance of influence (power)
- Living a centered versus balanced life (centering)
- Finding your unique trajectory (focusing)
- Assessing your spiritual vitality (auditing)

Under "Hand," you will be given practices, processes, procedures, methodologies, tactics, and strategies that will help you become a more effective leader, regardless of the number of people you lead. When the head and the heart are aligned—the beingness of our leadership—then the hand will produce God-honoring results. This section deals with the doingness of our leadership, the how-to of leadership.

---

[1]   Proverbs 4:23.

- How to come to terms with being a leader (leading)
- How to draw out unrealized potential (realizing)
- How to identify emerging leaders (recruiting)
- How to ask the right questions (interviewing)
- How to leverage temperament and leadership style (profiling)
- How to develop and train leaders (developing)
- How to mentor and be mentored (mentoring)
- How to develop a strategic plan (planning)
- How to use framing to solve problems (framing)
- How to establish goals to reach desired objectives (projecting)
- How to communicate effectively (communicating)
- How to solve problems effectively and efficiently (solving)
- How to resolve personal conflicts (resolving)
- How to motivate people to excel (motivating)
- How to focus on what you can influence (influencing)
- How to mobilize a team to meet any challenge (mobilizing)

Each chapter includes questions that will help you think through your leadership and how you intend to implement that leadership. These questions will compel you to think, reflect, and act in such a way that others will want to follow you. At the end of each chapter, I provide a recommended resource for your further understanding and development. Obviously, resources abound for the inquiring mind. The ones I have chosen represent my personal selection for the topic addressed. The chapters that follow represent my best understanding about leadership.

So why is leadership so important to me? Why do I feel compelled to offer my understanding of how to be and how to do leadership? What drives me to share what I have learned about leadership over seven decades? My personal life mandate urges me to do so.

My biblical purpose is to live with abandon, fulfilling the mandate God has given me. My mandate is to live in such a way as to exemplify and model Christlikeness in all I think, say, and do. The hills I will die on include fidelity to my personal relationship with Christ and my loyalty and faithfulness to him, faith as the saving grace of the gospel in all its implications, even if it takes me to uncomfortable places, family in striving to be and do what serves their best interests, and focus on God's purposes for my life in alignment with what he has called me to be and do. I seek to tune my heart to the heart of God and live accordingly. The Bible is my sole foundation, and I submit to its authority for faith and practice. My objective is to model the character of Christ and leave a pleasing aroma in the nostrils of all who come within my sphere of influence.

My life purpose is to influence leaders and intentional followers, directly and indirectly, to live all out for Christ, to facilitate a process to determine how God has wired them, to help them align their lives according to God's predetermined plans, to encourage them to become proactive partners in God's purposes and redemptive activity, and to exhort them to live a legacy worth leaving in the lives of others.

My committed passion is to help men and women realize their God-given potential in Christ and to develop to the fullest their God-given gifts, abilities, and capacities for godly leadership from the inside out and within legitimate limitations, such as temperament, aptitude, and maturity. My primary sphere of influence will be leaders. My secondary context will be men and women who are searching for clarity regarding the purpose, focus, and foundation for their lives.

The major role that will provide the platform for my life's purpose is one in which I'm allowed to focus my energies in investing in the lives of budding leaders in the process of becoming yet-not-arrived and malleable leaders who have the potential for greater purposes but do not have clarity or understanding on how to realize their full potential in Christ. This role will allow me to cultivate relationships with these leaders through the avenues of networking, teaching, writing, and mentoring one-on-one, in small groups and workshop settings, and exposing these leaders to leadership development concepts, values, principles, and practices. My spiritual gifts exercised in these settings find their primary application in the word-cluster gifts, including teaching, exhortation, and leadership. Less dominant but observable are the spiritual gifts of word of wisdom, discerning of spirits, and gifts of governments.

My unique methodologies find their roots in essentially five major ministry insights that have thematically repeated themselves over time in my ministry experience.

- Effective godly leadership flows from being, is a matter of the heart, and is primarily character-centered and secondarily skill-centered. Skills are the tools of effective leadership; character is the power of effective leadership.
- Lasting behavioral change that brings glory to God begins with the heart in general and our core belief system in particular. Satan's battlefield has always been the heart. What we store in our hearts will evidence itself in our behavior. Our central beliefs establish our core values, our core values inform our worldview, our worldview conditions our motives, and our motives energize our behavior.
- Authentic spirituality is a prerequisite for godly leadership and is produced when we tune our lives to God's standards of excellence. Its vitality comes from living our lives for an audience of One.
- Effective godly leadership is developed over a lifetime, is exercised through our God-given passion and giftedness, finds its source and authority in God, is built on biblical principles and values, and is practiced in culturally sensitive ways.
- The only legacy worth leaving is the godly legacy we live out daily and leave in the lives of others. Legacy is the sweet-smelling aroma that lingers in the lives of others long after we're gone from this earth.

These major ministry insights influence the cultivation of my network of relationships, the style of my teaching, the foci of my writing, and the emphases of my mentoring activities.

I intend to act faithfully through a commitment to acting in accordance with my core values, by leveraging my natural strengths, by finding appropriate expression for my personality temperament, and by exercising my leadership style in appropriate and life-giving ways.

I will exercise my mandate through my strengths, which include learner, activator, achiever, input, belief, relater, responsibility, command, focus, self-assurance, and strategic.

I also will leverage my mandate through my personality temperament (introversion, intuitive, thinking, judging—INTJ) and my primary leadership style of passion and mission, my secondary leadership style of corporate and causal, and my team leadership style of tactical engagement.

I will seek to live by my core values of devotion to God, a keeper of my promises, a seeker of biblical truth, a loyal servant, a man of integrity, faithfulness to my family, a lifelong learner, a biblically centered leader, one who submits to the authority of the Bible, one who is committed to responsible behavior, and a man of strength and honor.

Finally, I desire to use my acquired skills of biblical understanding, strategic planning, organization, implementation, leadership, development, mentoring, disciplining, communication, focused intensity, and spiritual guidance to further God's redemptive purposes in the world.

I hope that this brief introduction will encourage you to read and apply what follows. I honestly believe you will become a better leader by taking to heart and applying what is contained in this book.

HEAD

PRIORITIZING (WHERE AND WHEN TO ENGAGE)

Western culture has redefined *tolerance* as unconditional acceptance and affirmation.

Anything shy of total, unqualified acceptance and affirmation of the opinion, ideology, personal perspective, or lifestyle choices of another is labeled as intolerance.

The true definition of tolerance, however, is withholding whatever power you have against what you find objectionable. This means that we withhold whatever influence we can bring to bear on an issue for a more prudent engagement, a higher priority, or an assessment that opposing the issue will cause more damage than good. The power we are withholding may be the authority we have, the resources at our disposal, the network of influential contacts we can employ, the status we hold, the reputation we enjoy, or the knowledge we possess.

Every conflict, difference of opinion, or assault on our beliefs and values requires wisdom to determine whether to engage with whatever power we have available. The ancient scriptures give us guidance when they remind us to be wise, to evaluate the circumstances, and to assess the possible outcomes of engagement. We can choose not to make an issue of the matter for the sake of peace, grace, or forbearance.

If we choose to engage, we must always clothe ourselves with compassion, kindness, humility, gentleness, and patience. For those of us in the faith, we must "Always be prepared to give an answer to everyone who asks you to give the reason for the hope that you have. But do this with gentleness and respect, keeping a clear conscience, so that those who speak maliciously against your good behavior in Christ may be ashamed of their slander."[2]

Every effective leader of character has determined, in advance, which hills to die on, which hills to bleed on, and which hills not to climb at all. Doing so provides a framework of knowing when to engage, regardless of the circumstances; when to engage in consideration of the circumstances; and when to withhold engagement, despite the circumstances.

HILLS TO DIE ON

You cannot die on every hill. Dying may not require your life, but it may require something just as permanent or painful. Choosing to die on a hill may mean that you are willing to embrace the consequences even if it means you will lose the goodwill of others, marginalize your advancement prospects, or even lose your position, ranking, or job. The hill I choose to die on may not require my life, but it may require sacrificing popularity, acclaim, prestige, acceptance, or affirmation. It may require that I set aside my dreams and aspirations for a higher value. It may mean I may be marginalized or even ostracized.

Which hills are worth dying on?

> First, they should be few.
> Second, they should ensure laws, divine and secular, will not be violated.
> Third, they should honor our faith.
> Fourth, they should uphold our central beliefs and values. In other words, the matter is too important to

---

[2]   1 Peter 3:15.

ignore because it would mean that your character (or faith) is compromised.

Fifth, they should protect the defenseless, the unloved, and the marginalized.

These hills are not always a matter of public engagement. They may be a private or personal commitment, such as a commitment to live out certain beliefs and values, having decided which ones are nonnegotiable.

They may include putting the welfare and well-being of our families as our highest priority, in that we will never compromise this commitment for any reason.

They may include a commitment to submit to some cause, people group, or belief system that will stand in authority over our lives, informing and conditioning what we do.

HILLS TO BLEED ON

You cannot bleed on every hill. If you bleed on too many hills, you will "die" prematurely. I have known people who make an issue of every issue. It isn't long before whatever they say is automatically discounted, regardless of its importance. If you make an issue of every issue, no one will take seriously any issue you have made an issue. "For there is a proper time and procedure for every matter, though a man's misery weighs heavily upon him."[3]

"Hills to bleed on" is a metaphor for issues and concerns for which we are willing to take a stand, given the circumstances. They are situational in nature and change in terms of how we will respond. Environmental factors condition whether we choose to say something or do something. Given the alignment and significance of the contributing factors, we may choose to engage but are not willing to "die" for the issue. These issues are selected based on their importance, how they affect and/or their effect, and whether not engaging will give tacit approval to the outcome of the event or circumstance.

---

[3] Ecclesiastes 8:5–6.

One day you may choose to engage the issue, while at other times you may choose not to engage. This does not mean you are hypocritical or a "weather vane," moving in a direction of prevailing sentiment or political correctness. It simply means that you have measured the circumstance or event and have chosen that it is not a hill to bleed on. At other times, the circumstance or event may be a hill to bleed on; that is, worth risking your reputation, negatively impacting your relationships, or to losing respect or esteem.

In any case, choosing a hill to bleed on requires wisdom and the leading and/or conviction of the Holy Spirit. Hills to bleed on are not a matter of personal choice or feeling of obligation. Hills to bleed on are stimulated and instigated by the Lord, are energized by divine compulsion, and are engaged because you are led to do so by the Lord.

HILLS NOT TO CLIMB

There are many hills we are not called to climb. They may be important, but are they urgent? I would suggest that there are far more hills not to climb than you may know. This does not mean that the matters before you are not important or worth consideration. It simply means that you are not the one called to address it. The issue or concern is someone else's hill to die on or bleed on.

The intrinsic worth of the issue may be significant, but you are not the one to deal with it. You may hold certain convictions about it, may disagree or agree with it, may have something to contribute regarding it but have decided it is a hill you will not climb. Reasons for this conclusion may be decisions you made regarding the hills to die on or bleed on beforehand. This is not one of them. Or the criteria for engagement, which you have decided beforehand, is not met. Or engagement in this situation will do more damage than constructive help.

If a situation arises where you are trying to decide what to do, the following criteria might be considered.

1. Is it a hill I have already decided to die on?

2. Is it a hill I am prepared and led to bleed on?
3. Is it a hill someone else should die on or bleed on?
4. Is it a hill I have already decided not to climb?
5. Is it majoring in minors?

Each man and woman must decide for themselves which hills they will die on, which hills they will bleed on, and which hills are not to be climbed at all. Over the course of your life, these will change.

As for me I have decided which hills I will die on.

- My faith—the gospel and its obligations (Titus 2:11–14)
- My family—responsibility for their well-being (1 Timothy 5:8)
- My focus—my life purpose (Ephesians 2:8–10)
- My fidelity—the Bible and its authority (2 Timothy 3:16–17)

The hills I will bleed on will be the hills God calls me to bleed on. My hills will be different from your hills. The hills I will bleed on will be his hills and not my hills.

The hills not worth climbing are everything else. I have learned over time—I am in my sixties now—that I was dying on too many hills. The hills I was bleeding on were my hills and not his hills, and the hills I was not to climb at all were far more than I originally thought.

QUESTIONS TO PONDER

Which hills are you prepared to die on?

Which hills will you consider bleeding on if the circumstances warrant?

Which hills are not worth climbing?

RECOMMENDED RESOURCE

God First: Setting Life's Priorities (2016) by Bryan G. Sibley, MD

MARGIN (PROVIDING MARGIN FOR GROWTH)

> Now listen, you who say, "Today or tomorrow we will go to this or that city, spend a year there, carry on business and make money." Why, you do not even know what will happen tomorrow. What is your life? You are a mist that appears for a little while and then vanishes. Instead, you ought to say, "If it is the Lord's will, we will live and do this or that." As it is, you boast and brag. All such boasting is evil. Anyone, then, who knows the good he ought to do and doesn't do it, sins. (James 4:13–17)

Many of us are living hectic lives with little or no time to accommodate unexpected requests for our attention or engagement or to address the things that are important but not critical. There is no margin for such things. We are already at our maximum.

We bristle at any new demand made upon us. We become irritated at the audacity of anyone making such a request. "Don't they understand I am at my limit?"

We are living a "herniated disk" existence, in which any petition for our time is experienced as pain.

One of the more painful ailments is a herniated disk. When someone has a herniated disk, pain can be felt wherever the body is touched.

According to Mayo Clinic staff, a herniated disk refers to a problem with one of the rubbery cushions (disks) between the individual bones (vertebrae) that stack up to make your spine. A spinal disk is a little like a jelly doughnut, with a softer center encased within a tougher exterior. Sometimes called a slipped disk or a ruptured disk, a herniated disk occurs when some of the softer "jelly" pushes out through a crack in the tougher exterior.

The symptoms may include arm and leg pain, numbness or tingling, and muscle weakness served by the affected nerves. In fact, touching just about any part of the body causes one to wince.

Many of us live in a chronic state of busyness, with little time for spontaneity or space to enjoy the abundant life promised in scripture. In effect, we experience a "herniated disk" existence, in which any additional responsibility, obligation, commitment, expectation, or requirement is felt as added pain.

We know when we are living a "herniated" existence when a simple request or an unplanned or unexpected event pushes us over the edge. Our response is out of proportion to the circumstance. We become irritated or lash out at the request, feeling the pain of not having the space in our busy lives to respond. We resent the intrusion, and we let others know we resent it.

For instance:

- Our spouse asks us to take care of something that wasn't on the list of things we planned to do.
- Our son or daughter asks us to spend some time with him/her when we had hoped to rest after a particularly stressful day.
- Our pastor calls us to ask us to take on a new role or task that we know will demand time we don't have.
- Our small group requires our presence every other week for two hours and feels like yet another commitment for which we don't have time, given our busy schedules.
- Our boss asks us to take on an additional responsibility that is not in our job description.

We just can't seem to get to the things that we enjoy the most or that breathes life into our harried existence. We feel like the world is pushing in on us with demands we feel we cannot meet. We resent the intrusion. There is no time for these things, no room in our lives, no space to accommodate one more thing. Every new demand is viewed larger than it really is.

Dr. Richard Swenson defines *margin* as the distance or space between our load and our limits.[4] He identifies several stressors that can lead to overload, including change, mobility, expectations, time pressure, work, control, fear, relationships, competition, frustration, and anger. So, what is meant by our limits and our load?

Our limits include available time, innate and acquired ability, capacity, intellect, emotional stability, stress level, stage of life, physical health, and personality temperament.

Our load is represented by our current responsibilities, obligations, commitments, life circumstances, requirements, pledges, promises, duties, burdens, and liabilities.

When there is no margin in our lives, our load overwhelms our limits, and we are living a herniated life. Margin is that free space that can be accessed to accommodate the unexpected, the things we love to do but aren't critical, the stuff we want to do but rarely have the time to do, and the reasonable expectations of others that improve relationships.

So, how do we create margin in our lives? How do we make room in an already demanding schedule? How do we generate space for the unexpected?

It has been said that nature abhors a vacuum. In other words, when a vacuum exists, things cascade in to fill it. When margin exists in our lives, we need to resist the temptation to fill it immediately with something we haven't had room for up until now.

Margin is free space for worthwhile opportunities of a temporary nature that will not take up permanent residence, thereby diminishing

---

[4]   Richard A. Swenson, *Restoring Emotional, Physical, Financial, and Time Reserves to Overloaded Lives* (Colorado Springs: NavPress, 2004), 55.

our ability for any future opportunity. We need to be judicious on when, why, where, what, and how we temporarily use up this valuable space.

First things first: How do we create margin in our lives?

There is no shortcut; margin can be created only by elimination of something we are already doing. Eliminating behaviors to make room for margin takes discipline, commitment, and courage. Some habits are difficult to change and will take time.

The first thing to go is any dysfunctional activity that robs us of our precious time. What behaviors are we engaged in that are time wasters, unhealthy, corrupting, or sinful that steal what little discretionary time we have available? What habits have we nurtured that need to be reined in? What hobbies do we have that time expended doing them are beyond reasonable limits? What activities are we engaged in that are not healthy or that are out of control?

The second thing to go are those things that are unhealthy and impair our physical health, interfere with getting the sleep we need, prevent us from enjoying periods of rest and relaxation, hinder us from establishing and sustaining meaningful relationships and friendships, and thwart our spiritual development and maturation.

As a side note, I find it ironic that we always seem to find the time for things we really want to do, even when those things are not good for us.

The final thing to go is the notion that our jobs are our identity or the place where we derive our value. It is not what you do that determines who you are. It is who you are in Christ that should inform, condition, and qualify what you do. Your job is the gift God gives you to provide for your needs and have some left over to give to the needy. Workaholism is a dysfunctional pattern that sucks up what little margin we have let alone and prevents us from other things that really matter.

Second: What will help us create margin in our lives? What will help us to determine what should be eliminated to produce margin in our lives? What will inform the tough decisions we might have to make to create margin in our lives?

Answers to these important and life-changing questions begin with prayer, self-reflection, honest evaluation, guidance from respected mentors, and heartfelt assessment. This personal appraisal must be informed and conditioned by some respected authority that will bring cohesion, consistency, coherence, and congruence to our lives. I believe that authority is God and his Word, the Bible.

One worthwhile activity will help us determine what to eliminate in our lives to create margin. That activity is to discover our God-given and ordained trajectory, which will clarify our unique journey and destiny.

We were brought into this world by God's sovereign initiative and design.[5] We are here to fulfill his divine purpose that he determined in advance for each of us, uniquely.[6]

When we have clarity regarding our personal life mandate, our calling, we will have the confidence we need to say no to some things and yes to others.

Our personal life mandate consists of the following elements:

- Our biblical purpose (our beingness, which provides the energy we need)
- Our life purpose (our doingness, which provides the path we are to travel)
- Our committed passion (the people group we are called to serve or the cause we are called to embrace)
- Our nonnegotiables in any role we assume (those things that must be present in any situation for us to thrive)
- Our unique methodologies (our tool kit that helps us effectively do what we are called to do)
- Our ultimate contributions (the legacy we will leave when God calls us home)

In summary, margin is needed in our lives to accommodate unexpected or unplanned requests for our time that matter, that are important, that correlate with our calling, and that reflect God's priorities. Margin can only be produced by elimination of things that

---

5   Psalm 139:1–18.
6   Ephesians 2:10.

are not necessary; that are sinful, dysfunctional, or unhealthy; that are not hills to die on or bleed on; and are not in accordance with our personal life mandate.

QUESTIONS TO PONDER

What is your current load?

What are your current limits?

What do you need to keep doing, change doing, stop doing, and start doing?

RECOMMENDED RESOURCE

Margin: Restoring Emotional, Physical, Financial, and Time Reserves to Overloaded Lives (2004) by Richard A. Swenson, MD

DISCERNING (MAKING GOOD DECISIONS)

An ancient writer once said, "Who is like the wise man? Who knows the explanation of things? Wisdom brightens a man's face and changes its hard appearance … and the wise heart will know the proper time and procedure. For there is a proper time and procedure for every matter, though a man's misery weighs heavily upon him."[7]

How many wise leaders do you know? When I was executive pastor of a large church in Southern California, a prominent internationally renowned church leader visited our church. I asked him what he thought was the biggest problem facing leaders for the foreseeable future. His answer came quickly and consisted of one word: *discernment.*

How does a leader discern the right course of action, decide between two equally viable options, be objectively informed by divergent perspectives, suspend his/her own predispositions and biases to hear different voices, and consult his/her inner convictions before deciding? To a great degree, their intuition, enlightened by insight, will help them make wise decisions.

Three levels of insight of increasing complexity are possible. These levels are used by leaders to make decisions: the information level, the knowledge level, and the wisdom level.

Many of us are living at the information level, which is simply the

---

[7]   Ecclesiastes 8:1, 5, 6.

ordered understanding of raw data. We do not give enough time to reflection leading to comprehension. The tyranny of the urgent, the frenzied activity of our daily lives, and the constant bombardment of data (TV, faxes, newspapers, magazines, internet, email, radio, audio tapes, videos, podcasts, webinars, superficial conversations, etc.) rob us of an ordered analysis of our world. We operate off sound bites instead of measured and thoughtful examination.

Many others are stuck at the knowledge level, satisfied with the acquisition and accumulation of information ordered in such a way as to produce an intellectual grasp of the essentials, enough to converse intelligently on the subject but little more. We acquire competencies analyzing data and applying rubrics to tease out nuggets that will hopefully propel us into a preferable outcome or attainment of a sought-after goal. The trouble with remaining at this level is that our mental comprehension doesn't move on to applied wisdom.

We need to move to the wisdom level by prioritizing the acquisition and accumulation of knowledge into wisdom. Wisdom is an internal quality developed over time, established by a congruent belief system, conditioned by a core value system, informed by an integrated worldview, and honed through experience. Learned methods, processes, systems, and strategies are the tools we use, but it is wisdom that provides discernment in their application.

For instance, the internet offers access to information on almost every topic imaginable. Any person can acquire information on a given topic, recast it in his/her own words, and present the information as if it were his/her own. When we process that information, comprehend its significance, visualize its application, and apply that knowledge to events, situations, or circumstances, we are operating at a knowledge level. Weighing the significance of information, analyzing the specifics of a body of information, synthesizing it with other related information, evaluating the importance of the information, and making informed judgments regarding the utility of the information is operating at a wisdom level.

As an example, in Exodus 20 we are exposed to information—the existence of ten commandments. We develop a knowledge about them when, through study and reflection, we comprehend their meaning (i.e., the first four commandments address our relationship with God, and the remaining six commandments address our relationship with others). Knowledge becomes wisdom when we understand the commandments' implications to us individually, and we personally apply them to our lives as we process them through a belief system that has established our values.

In the popular movie *Jurassic Park*, the proprietor of the park, John Hammond, presides over a lunch with invited guests who have just witnessed the amazing existence of dinosaurs created in a lab and now roaming the grounds. John is criticized by Malcolm, a skeptic who questions the entire enterprise.[8]

> MALCOLM: The problem with scientific power you've used is it didn't require any discipline to attain it. You read what others had done and you took the next step. You didn't earn the knowledge yourselves, so you don't take the responsibility for it. You stood on the shoulders of geniuses to accomplish something as fast as you could, and before you knew what you had, you patented it, packaged it, slapped it in a plastic lunch box, and now you want to sell it.

> HAMMOND: You don't give us our due credit. Our scientists have done things no one could ever do before.

> MALCOLM: Your scientists were so preoccupied with whether or not they could that they didn't stop to think if they should. Science can create pesticides, but it can't tell us not to use them. Science can make a nuclear reactor, but it can't tell us not to build it!

---

[8]   Michael Crichton, *Jurassic Park*. Movie directed by Steven Spielberg. Amblin Entertainment: Universal Pictures, 1993.

In summary, then, information is the ordered understanding of raw data. Knowledge is meaning derived through study, reflection, and comprehension. Wisdom is knowledge applied based on one's core beliefs and values. There is a vast distance between having knowledge about something and having personal knowledge of something. The bridge from one to the other is wisdom.

TYPES OF WISDOM

There are four types of wisdom: natural wisdom, worldly wisdom, the gift of wisdom, and godly wisdom.

Natural wisdom finds its source in the sum of life's experiences. It can be inherited. Some people are born wise or have the natural capacity to draw wisdom from their surroundings. It can be learned from others, life circumstances, trial and error, observation, or experience.

Natural wisdom is another name for common sense. When Paul and his traveling companions were in Ephesus, they created an uproar when they questioned the efficacy of gods. The chief secretary of Ephesus quelled the crowd by using common sense.[9]

Worldly wisdom seeks insight apart from God. In fact, it opposes the purposes of God. Inspired by the enemy, it seeks to undermine God's redemptive purposes and calls his existence into question.[10] Thwarting any divine initiative and questioning biblical principles and values is the aim. In our society today, we see examples of factions intentionally undermining Christianity using worldly wisdom. Secular humanism is an example of this type of wisdom.

The gift of wisdom is a spiritual gift from God.[11] People who possess this gift have an intimate understanding of God's Word and his commandments, which results in holy and upright living. It speaks into the life of individuals or a specific situation with great understanding and a biblically informed perspective. Its goal is to guide others toward a life of godliness.

---

[9] Acts 19:35–41.
[10] James 3:11–15; 1 Corinthians 3:19–20; Colossians 2:23.
[11] 1 Corinthians 12:8; Acts 6:3.

Godly wisdom sees life from God's perspective. A biblical worldview informs this wisdom and draws its clarity from the scriptures. It is the result of walking closely with God, seeing the world as God sees it, understanding the underlying influences that give rise to behavior, and drawing accurate observations. It is based on biblically based beliefs and values.[12] We are encouraged to ask for this wisdom.[13] Exercise of this wisdom produces Bible-centered words and actions.

CHARACTERISTICS OF GODLY WISDOM

Godly wisdom is centered in Christ[14] and understood and discerned through the Spirit.[15] It consists of the knowledge of his will,[16] requires an exercise of faith,[17] is not self-centered,[18] is based on the Word of God,[19] and is perfected in obedience.[20]

Godly wisdom is cultivated by going to the Bible with intentionality, listening for God's "still small voice," and journaling your findings. Reading and rereading the books of Proverbs and Ecclesiastes will help develop godly wisdom. It is also a by-product of allowing the Bible to challenge and influence your core beliefs and values.

Calibrate your attitudes and worldview by the unchanging standard of God's Word. Process what you hear, read, and see through a biblical perspective. Personally apply the Bible by way of meditation and purposeful reflection.

Finally, ask for it. Believe and don't doubt. Evaluate it. Act on it.

---

12 Colossians 3:16; James 3:17.
13 James 1:5.
14 1 Corinthians 1:30; Colossians 2:2–3.
15 1 Corinthians 2:6–16.
16 Colossians 1:9; Ephesians 1:8–10.
17 James 1:5–7.
18 James 3:13–17.
19 Colossians 1:28; 3:16; Psalm 11:10.
20 Deuteronomy 4:6; Jeremiah 8:8–9; Proverbs 10:8.

QUESTIONS TO PONDER

What level of insight do you employ?

What type of wisdom do you practice?

What informs and conditions your thought process?

How discerning are you?

What sources and resources do you use to make decisions?

What ethical system influences your decisions?

RECOMMENDED RESOURCE

Decision Making and the Will of God: A Biblical Alternative to the Traditional View (2004) by Gary Friesen and J. Robin Maxson

MEDITATING (FILLING YOUR MIND WITH GOD'S MIND)

A man approached a speaker and said, "You Christians are all brainwashed." The speaker replied, "I think we are all brainwashed to a degree. The important thing is that we Christians choose what we want to wash our brains with."

Meditation is a lost art for many Christians, but the practice needs to be cultivated again. Meditation is the bridge we cross to personal application of general biblical principles. J. I. Packer, in his classic book, *Knowing God* (1973), makes two insightful observations.

> One can know a great deal about God without much knowledge of him. One can know a great deal about godliness without much knowledge of God.[21]

We have great access to books about God—theology, commentaries, handbooks, language resources, topical Bibles, etc. J. I. Packer concludes:

> All very fine—yet interest in theology, and knowledge about God, and the capacity to think clearly and talk

---

[21] J. I. Packer, *Knowing God* (Downers Grove: InterVarsity Press, 1973), 21–22.

well on Christian themes, is not at all the same thing as knowing him.[22]

We tend to shortcut the learning process by reading and using how-to books on every theme under the sun. This prechewed, predigested diet from leading scholars or contemporary expositors of the Word rob us of the joy of searching his Word for ourselves so that we can hear his still small voice and apply his principles firsthand, rather than secondhand.

We are on a personal spiritual journey. How many of us long to be experienced travelers, yet seem satisfied with reading about other people's journeys instead of enjoying our own? J. I. Packer goes on to describe the four basic characteristics of people who have a knowledge *of* God versus a knowledge *about* God.

- Those who know God have great energy for God.
- Those who know God have great thoughts of God.
- Those who know God show great boldness for God.
- Those who know God have great contentment in God.

It may be that the reason we have lost the art of meditation is because our idea of success in this area is based on false expectations. We expected emotional exhilaration and were disappointed because we didn't feel a difference. We weren't stimulated or excited, so we gave up.

Archibald D. Hart wrote a book on *Adrenaline and Stress* (1995).[23] He made the following comment in an article for *Preaching Today*:

> A constant state of adrenalin arousal, although physically damaging, is often experienced as pleasant excitement and stimulation. And it is this that makes it most dangerous, because we can come to think of the arousal state as "normal" and to depend on the

---

22   Ibid., 22.

23   Archibald D. Hart, *Adrenaline and Stress: The Exciting New Breakthrough That Helps You Overcome Stress Damage* (Nashville: Thomas Nelson Publishers, 1995).

high it gives us to get anything accomplished. I believe there is a corresponding spiritual danger. Becoming dependent on adrenalin arousal for the good feelings of life can create an association between spirituality and high arousal. In other words, one doesn't feel "spiritual" unless one is being stimulated by adrenalin arousal. Many expressions of spirituality have become linked to adrenalin arousal, and this can be very harmful. A great many of the true saints of God have found their peak spiritual experiences in quietness and solitude. But many modern "saints" look for it only in exciting challenges or emotional catharsis.[24]

So, what is meditation? We could not find a better definition than the one proposed by Packer. "Meditation is the activity of calling to mind, and thinking over, and dwelling on, and applying to oneself, the various things that one knows about the works and ways and purposes and promises of God. It is the activity of holy thought, consciously performed in the presence of God, under the eye of God, by the help of God, as a means of communion with God. Its purpose is to clear one's mental and spiritual vision of God, and to let its truth make its full and proper impact on one's mind and heart."[25] Meditation is the regular filling of your mind with the thoughts of God and godly thoughts.

Finally, brothers, whatever is true, whatever is noble, whatever is right, whatever is pure, whatever is lovely, whatever is admirable if anything is excellent or praiseworthy think about such things.[26]

Why should I meditate? Richard J. Foster, in his highly acclaimed book *Celebration of Discipline* (2002),[27] remarked on how busy activity can keep us from needed contemplation on God's truth. "In

[24] Archibald D. Hart, "Adrenalin-Fed Spirituality," *Preaching Today*, June 1998. http://www.preachingtoday.com/illustrations/1998/june/4430.html.

[25] J. I. Packer, *Knowing God* (Downers Grove: InterVarsity Press, 1973), 18–19.

[26] Philippians 4:8.

[27] Richard J. Foster, *Celebration of Discipline: The Path to Spiritual Growth* (San Francisco: Harper Publishers, 2002).

contemporary society our Adversary majors in three things: noise, hurry, and crowds. If he can keep us engaged in 'muchness' and 'manyness', he will rest satisfied."[28] He further quotes psychiatrist C. G. Jung: "Hurry is not of the Devil; it is the Devil."[29]

Why meditate? Because the Word of God encourages us to do so. We are to meditate on his Word, day and night.[30] Our meditation is pleasing to the Lord.[31] Our meditation makes us aware of how we demonstrate our love for him through obedience to his Word.[32] Our meditation helps us focus on what is important to God.[33] Our meditation gives us an eternal perspective.[34]

Dietrich Bonhoeffer, in *The Way to Freedom* (1966),[35] identifies three compelling reasons to meditate on God and his Word:

1. Because we are Christians who need to penetrate more deeply into the knowledge of the Word of God for establishing a firm foundation.
2. Because we need a firm discipline of prayer, the day's first service to God, and his opportunity to register his presence in our hearts.
3. Because we need help against the unseemly haste and disquiet that endangers our work as pastors. Truly devoted service each day comes only from the peace of the Word of God.

Neil Anderson, author of *Bondage Breaker* (2006),[36] declared it's not what you do that determines who you are. It's what you are that

---

28   Ibid., 15.
29   Ibid., 15.
30   Psalm 1:2.
31   Psalm 19:14.
32   Joshua 1:8.
33   Philippians 4:8.
34   Colossians 3:2.
35   Dietrich Bonhoeffer, *The Way to Freedom* (New York: HarperCollins Publishers, 1966).
36   Neil Anderson, *Bondage Breaker* (Eugene: Harvest House Publishers, 2006).

determines what you do. What we are, our character, determines our behavior. Our character is made up of our beliefs, values, attitudes, and motives. Our character becomes Christlike through meditation and application, borne of our precious time with God.[37]

As Christians, people should see Christ in us. Our actions speak louder than our words. Our actions reflect our characters.

What can we expect from meditation? Bonhoeffer suggests that we want to rise from meditation different from what we were when we sat down to do it. We want to meet Christ in his Word. His fellowship, his help, and his direction for the day through his Word—that is his aim.

Foster describes the following as our goals: a sense of balance in our lives, an ability to rest and take time to enjoy beauty, and an ability to pace ourselves. Meditation should produce a knowledge *of* God and not a knowledge *about* God. Over time our meditation will transform our characters. God's presence will become increasingly real to us as our relationships with him deepen. Our demeanors will reflect the glory of God as we consciously and unconsciously manifest his excellence in our lives.

What can we expect? We can expect purification,[38] invigoration,[39] endurance,[40] transformation,[41] and renewal.[42]

How should you meditate? Find a place that is quiet and free from interruption. Stay away from the telephone. Find a place that is peaceful, that typifies contentment for you. Try to find one designated place rather than hunting for a different spot each day. Foster comments that posture makes no difference at all; you can meditate and pray anywhere, any time, and in any position. He goes on to say, however, that the body, the mind, and the spirit are inseparable. Not only does outward

---

[37] 2 Corinthians 3:18.

[38] Psalm 51:10.

[39] Psalm 103:5.

[40] Isaiah 40:31.

[41] Romans 12:2.

[42] 2 Corinthians 4:16.

posture reflect the inward state, but it also can help to nurture the inner attitude of prayer.

The Bible describes everything from lying prostrate on the floor to standing with hands and head lifted toward the heavens. The best approach is to find a position that is most comfortable and the least distracting. The aim is "to center the attention of the body, the emotions, the mind and the spirit upon 'the glory of God in the face of Christ.'"[43]

Biblical meditation shapes our prayers, disciplines our thoughts, and makes us conscious of our fellowship with God. Bonhoeffer's words are helpful at this point.

> The Word of Scripture should never stop sounding in your ears and working in you all day long love. Just as you do not analyze the words of someone you love but accept them as they are said to you, accept the word of Scripture and ponder it in your heart. "Do not look for new thoughts and connections in the text, as you would if you were preaching! Do not ask 'How shall I pass this on?' but "What does it say to me?" Then ponder this word long in your heart until it has gone right into you and taken possession of you.[44]

There are several types of biblical meditation you can adopt for your personal use.

Meditate on some aspect of creation. Choose something in the created order—tree, plant, bird, leaf, cloud—and ponder it carefully and prayerfully for five to ten minutes. God, who made the heavens and the earth, uses his creation to show us something of his glory and give us something of his life.

Foster states the "meditation upon Scripture becomes the central

---

43   2 Corinthians 4:6.
44   Dietrich Bonhoeffer, "Lectio Divina (Divine Reading)." *Selah Center*. January 2016. http://selahcenter.org/lectio-divina/.

reference point by which all meditations are kept in proper perspective."[45] Meditation on scripture centers on "internalizing and personalizing" the passage. Bonhoeffer recommended spending a whole week on a single text.

Take a single event, like the resurrection, or a parable, or a few verses, or even a single word, and allow it to take root in you. Use your five senses to live the experience (smell, hear, feel, see, taste, touch). You can encounter the living Christ in the event.

The objective of this exercise is to bring you into a deep inner communion with the Father, in which you look at him, and he looks at you. Picture and sense a place of beauty and peace (a forest and stream, flowers and birds, a lovely grassy knoll, a lush large meadow encircled by stately pines, a blue sky and light clouds).

Sense this place with all your senses. Sense the warm presence of the eternal Creator. Rest in his presence. Listen quietly, anticipating the unanticipated. Note carefully any instruction given. When it's time to leave, audibly thank the Lord for his goodness.

This exercise meditates upon the events of our time and seeks to perceive their significance. It's a process whereby we try to gain God's perspective through the lens of his Word. This form of meditation is best accomplished with the Bible in one hand and a newspaper or magazine in the other. Hold these events before God and ask for insight to discern where these things lead. Ask for guidance for anything you personally should be doing to be salt and light in our "decaying and dark world."

Select one or more of the specific exercises described above. Find a quiet location apart from others, and complete the meditation exercise.

As Foster remarks, "meditation is not a single act, nor can it be completed the way one completes the building of a chair. It is a way of life. You will be constantly learning and growing as you plumb the inner depths."[46] Welcome to an incredible journey! May God bless your

---

[45]   Richard J. Foster, *Celebration of Discipline: The Path to Spiritual Growth* (San Francisco: Harper, 1988), 29.

[46]   Ibid., 32.

efforts as you meditate upon him and bask in his glory. Maybe someone will come up to you one day and say, "Are you Jesus?"

The following resources will help you regarding meditation;

- Foster, Richard J. *Celebration of Discipline.* New York: Harper & Row, 1978.
- Packer, J. I. *Knowing God.* Illinois: InterVarsity Press, 1973.

QUESTIONS TO PONDER

When was the last time you heard the voice of God in your life?
When was the last time you took a spiritual retreat?
How will you make meditation a part of your routine?

RECOMMENDED RESOURCE

Christian Meditation: Experiencing the Presence of God (2005) by James Finley

PERCEIVING (GRASPING REALITY AND ADJUSTING EXPECTATIONS ACCORDINGLY)

Some people live in an alternate reality. Their narrative is fed by fictional perceptions of their own making. Basing our life or pursuits on this alternate reality produces expectations impossible to meet. If we base our perceptions on truth, however, and expectations are adjusted accordingly, the outcome is much more positive, depending, of course, on the dedication we have to pursuing a reality grounded in truth.

The Bible tells us the truth will set us free;[47] we must walk in truth;[48] truth dispels darkness;[49] and Jesus is the truth.[50] Our grasp of what is true is the best starting point of any initiative. If we engage an endeavor and proceed based on our perception of reality, not based on the truth, we will end up in places not originally planned, disappointed that we never reached our intended objective.

You may have heard the popular refrain "My perceptions are my reality." Such a thought may be true for that person, but if it is not

---

[47]   John 8:31–32.

[48]   2 John 4–5; 3 John 3–4.

[49]   1 John 1:6–7.

[50]   John 14:6–7.

based on truth, the person is living in an alternate reality with little relationship to true reality.

Let's look at a formula that helps describe the relationship between reality and expectations and the result they may produce.

$$S = \frac{R \text{ (Reality)}}{E \text{ (Expectations)}}$$

(Satisfaction)
(Significance)
(Success)

The degree to which we experience S depends on the relationship between R and E. Our perception of reality and the formulation of our expectations based on that reality is crucial to the sense of satisfaction or significance or success we enjoy.

Looking at satisfaction as the preferred outcome, the degree to which our expectations are less than or equal to reality will determine the degree to which we enjoy satisfaction.

Stay with me now—looking at the formula mathematically, we can see that if reality is met with expectations that either match or approach but do not exceed reality, we will enjoy satisfaction to its maximum.

- $S(1) = R(2)/E(2)$
- $S(2) = R(2)/E(1)$

If reality is met with expectations that exceed reality, we will experience less than a satisfactory outcome, to the degree our expectations exceed the reality.

- S (1/2) = R (1)/E (2)

What am I trying to say? Our grasp of reality versus our perceptions of reality will positively or negatively impact our expectations. In other words, our grasp of the truth is critical to enjoying a satisfactory outcome, a feeling of significance, or some measure of success.

If our reality is not based on the certainty of truth and instead is based on a misperception or falsehood, then our expectations will be unrealistic, practically unattainable, and essentially unrealized.

Contrary to popular opinion, our perceptions are not reality if they are not based on truth and facts. What we perceive to be true may be, in fact, a lie, false, or fiction. Living that way will only produce disappointment, despair, discouragement, and failure—an alternative reality that has no basis in true reality.

For instance, telling children that they can do anything if they simply put their minds to it and apply themselves is a misperception at best and a lie at worst. Expectations adjusted to this falsehood will result in utter frustration, adversely impact their self-esteem, and curtail their motivation going forward. We can become all we can become, based on our innate talents and wiring, the circumstances we experience, the legitimate limitations we encounter, and the opportunity that presents itself, if we apply ourselves accordingly.

Let's say we fully comprehend how God has wired us and that an opportunity presents itself that resonates with our wiring or falls within the realm of our potential. Our reality at this point is true, given the facts as we know them. Two options are possible:

1. We adjust our expectations to this reality and therefore have a reasonable chance to enjoy success in the pursuit of that reality.
2. We place expectations on ourselves that exceed reality, and therefore we will meet with disappointment and failure.

No matter how hard I try to apply myself, I will not become a mathematician. I struggled through high school with algebra, geometry, and trigonometry. I was never any good at it, no matter how hard I tried. Some people are gifted that way; not me. So, if I set my goal at becoming a mathematician, I am sure I would meet with little if any success. Being a stellar mathematician is not reality for me. I have other talents and gifts that I could pursue with a good chance of succeeding, based on my wiring.

Reality based on truth will help us determine the universe of possibilities for us. How you are wired provides the parameters for your universe of possibilities. Answers to the following questions will help determine the boundaries of your expectations.

- What is your life purpose?
- What is your committed passion?
- What are your natural talents and abilities?
- What are your spiritual gifts?
- What are your acquired skills?
- What is your personality temperament?
- What is your natural leadership style?
- What are your biblically informed beliefs and values?
- What are your life principles?
- What legacy do you hope to leave?
- What contributions do you hope to make?
- What will remain of value after you are gone?

Accurate and truthful answers to these questions will provide a solid foundation on which to build reality as to what is possible and what is not.

What can we learn from this?

It is very important that we know the facts, the truth of the matter, and that our grasp of reality is based on the truth. Otherwise, our misperceptions of reality will set an unrealistic threshold. Our expectations based on an unrealistic threshold will meet with failure. As God's Word reminds us, "the truth will set us free."[51]

---

[51] John 8:31–32.

QUESTIONS TO PONDER

Do you have a grasp of reality, or is your life based on fiction?

Are your expectations based on reality?

Given your innate and inborn abilities, what goals are realistic for you?

RECOMMENDED RESOURCE

Fool's Gold?: Discerning Truth in an Age of Error (2005) by John MacArthur and Contributors

TRANSITIONING (UNDERSTANDING BOUNDARY EVENTS THAT MOVE US TO THE NEXT THING)

Boundary events are transitional periods in our lives that move us from one phase of growth or development to the next. Most leaders move from establishing foundations, beginning in childhood; to preparation, where leaders pursue formal training; to contribution, where leaders exercise what they have learned in the laboratory we call work; to a place of multiplication, where their experiences have matured and can be leveraged for greater effectiveness within their spheres of influence.

Boundary events are precipitated and initiated by a circumstance, situation, or occasion, not all of which are positive. These events can be instigated by a crisis or transition, such as a new opportunity, being fired, a health crisis, being laid off, completion of one's education, midlife crisis, promotion, spiritual experience, an epiphany, an awakening, an accumulation of related circumstances, gradual discontent, failure, success, a challenge, significant change, new life stage, or a major change of perspective.

Research has shown that boundary events can last anywhere from two to three months to as long as six years. Regardless of the length of time or how they are brought into play, boundary events consist of essentially three stages: entry, evaluation, and exit.[52]

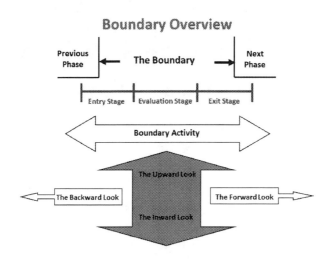

The entry stage is a period when leaders reflect on what just happened to them. They try to reconcile the events that led up to it to understand and connect the dots. This stage looks to the past and often is accompanied by grieving over the loss. Leaders may experience anger, disappointment, despair, and discouragement if the precipitating circumstances were unexpected or negative in nature. It is important to remember that this self-analysis will rarely, if at all, yield all the answers. Eventually, leaders come to terms with the circumstances, even though many questions about the circumstances remain unclear. Leaders finally reach a point where they realize "It is what it is." If the circumstances leading to the boundary event are perceived as positive (e.g., a promotion, new opportunity, the completion of a journey, etc.), then the reflection of the past is simply a period of encouragement, appreciation, sense of accomplishment, or achievement.

The evaluation stage consists of two periods of activity. The focus of this stage is the present, at which time they take an inward look

---

52   J. Robert Clinton, *Leadership Emergence Theory: A Self-Study Manual for Analyzing the Development of a Christian Leader* (Altadena: Barnabas Publishers, 1989), 305–306.

and may even look upward for spiritual guidance. The first period involves self-evaluation. Leaders take stock of what they have to offer. They assess their capabilities and capacity for the next phase of their journeys. They may even seek further assessment through nonformal means, such as using a coach, taking various instruments, preparing a personal historical timeline, gathering observations of others, attending self-help and self-management workshops or seminars, and/or seeking professional guidance. The objective is to gain clarity of their personal tool kits of gifts, talents, natural abilities, acquired competencies and skills, and lessons learned from their experiences.

Once the self-evaluation is complete, and leaders have an accurate grasp of what they have to offer, they may determine that there are some holes in their portfolios. They may seek further education, undergo coaching to learn a new competency or skill, seek professional career guidance, or acquire a mentor who can help them fill out their unrealized potential in anticipation of their next big step. This period might also include a personal audit in which they determine their life purpose, committed passion, nonnegotiables going forward, unique methodologies (their toolboxes), and ultimate contributions or legacies they hope to leave. This personal life mandate will serve as a filter through which they will process new opportunities to ensure that they are operating from their sweet spot.

The exit stage of the boundary event looks to the future. Leaders are ready to move on and embrace something new and different. They are ready to put past circumstances behind them and engage a new aspect of their journeys. They come out of their hunkered-down existence, ready to tackle the world but with a new commitment, a new focus, a new perspective, a new attitude, a new sense of hope, a new beginning, a new future. They will initiate action to find a new position, start a new business, or embrace a new vocation altogether. They will actively pursue new opportunities in alignment with their wiring and new trajectory.

In many cases the transition from evaluation to exit is not dramatic but incremental. It also may be true that leaders do not know they have transitioned from the evaluation to the exit stage until after it already has happened. Once they have exited and started afresh, the boundary event is concluded. Some leaders will experience multiple boundary events in their lives—a movement to calling, a movement to beingness versus doingness, a movement to legacy or ultimate contribution.

Knowing what and how boundary events operate will help leaders deal with the range of emotions they will experience while going through it. Such understanding will mediate confusion and help the leader understand what to expect and how to endure it. Boundary events serve to bring closure to recent experiences; deepen beliefs, values, and convictions; expand perspectives to see new things; and make decisions that will launch them into a new phase of their lives.

QUESTIONS TO PONDER

What boundary events have you experienced in the past?

What boundary event are you in right now? In what stage are you?

How have you processed (or how are you processing) your boundary event?

RECOMMENDED RESOURCE

Stuck!: Navigating Life and Leadership Transitions (2015) by Terry B. Walling

FINISHING (HOW TO AVOID BARRIERS AND FINISH WELL)

What compels a person to strive for excellence? What pushes a person to succeed? What motivates a person to do his/her best? Certainly, many motives might be in play, some laudable and others not so much. I believe that deep within every individual is a desire to finish well. Using grounded theory, a qualitative research methodology, J. Robert Clinton and his team of researchers studied the lives of Christian leaders—biblical, historical, and contemporary leaders—to ascertain how they finished the race. Over 3,800 case studies have underscored the findings. One of the startling facts is that only 30 percent finished well. According to Clinton, anecdotal evidence from today indicates that this ratio is probably generous. Probably less than one in three finishes well today.

Four types of finishes were defined in *Starting Well* by Richard Clinton and Paul Leavenworth (2012).[53] These finishes were used to analyze the case studies of biblical leaders, where enough data was available to determine how they finished.

---

[53] Paul Leavenworth and Richard Clinton, *Starting Well: Building a Strong Foundation for a Lifetime of Ministry* (CreateSpace Independent Publishing, 2012), 12–13.

- Cut off early: These leaders are taken out of leadership by assassination, killed in battle, prophetically denounced, or overthrown. Some of this activity was directly attributed to God. Some of these were positive, and others were negative (Abimelech, Samson, Absalom, Ahab, Josiah, John the Baptist, James).
- Finished poorly: These leaders were going downhill in the latter part of their ministry. This might be reflected in their personal relationships with God or in terms of their competency in ministry (Gideon, Samson, Eli, Saul, Solomon).
- Finished so-so: These leaders did fairly well but were limited in their ministries because of sin. They did not complete what God had for them, or they had some negative ramifications surrounding their lives and ministries, even though they personally walked with God (David, Jehoshaphat, Hezekiah).
- Finished well: These leaders were walking with God at the end of their lives. They contributed to God's purposes at a high level. They fulfilled what God had for them to do (Abraham, Job, Joseph, Joshua, Caleb, Samuel, Elijah, Jeremiah, Daniel, Jesus, John, Paul, Peter).

Dr. J. Robert Clinton defines *finishing well* as referring to reaching the end of one's life, having been faithful to the calling God has placed upon that life. It is about Christ followers being more passionate about Christ and his mission as they fulfilled their life purposes than they were at the beginning. It also entails a life that experiences the depth of God's grace and love. It is living out one's destiny and the making of one's unique and ultimate contribution in expanding God's kingdom.

How we *finish* is all about legacy—the aroma left in the lives of people who have come within our sphere of influence. Have I fulfilled my divinely ordained purpose? Have I made progress in leveraging my giftedness (spiritual gifts, natural abilities, and acquired skills) for eternal ends? Will the substance of my life leave a positive impact that will endure after I am gone? Although starting well is important, finishing well is crucial.

Within the soul of every human being God has placed a sense of the eternal that compels us to seek answers to the following questions, having to do with purpose, progress, and permanence.[54]

- Why am I here? Purpose
- Am I making any headway? Progress
- Will what I do have any lasting significance? Permanence

It also is true that God has wired us for three reasons—a cause to die for, a challenge to embrace, and loved ones to protect, just like our Lord. He had a cause to die for—the salvation of humankind. He had a challenge to embrace—the Crucifixion. And He had loved ones to protect—humankind.

Finishing well takes these matters into consideration. You are not an accident, a coincidence, a happenstance. You were on the heart of God before you ever came to be.[55] God indeed has plans for you and determined your purpose in advance of your birth.[56]

So the big question is, how will you finish? Tangential to this main question are the following questions: How will you be remembered? Who has been left better off because of you? If you left this world today, what type of finish would be true of you?

It is never too late to begin living a legacy worth leaving in the lives of others. What are you doing now to determine God's purpose for your life? What are you doing now to facilitate God's giftedness in you? What do you intend to do going forward to finish well?

If finishing well is a preferred objective of your life, what are the characteristics of people who finish well? What can we learn from biblical, historical, and contemporary Christian leaders that will help us to be able to finish well? When I am called home by the Lord, I hope to cross the finish line utterly exhausted, having given my all for kingdom purposes that matter, having set a model for my grandchildren to follow,

---

[54] Ecclesiastes 3:10–11.

[55] Psalm 139:1–18.

[56] Ephesians 2:10.

having acquitted myself with honor, so that I can lay my meager offering of dedicated service at his feet. Like Paul, I want to be able to say;

> For I am already being poured out like a drink offering, and the time has come for my departure. I have fought the good fight, I have finished the race, I have kept the faith. Now there is in store for me the crown of righteousness, which the Lord, the righteous Judge, will award to me on that day — and not only to me, but also to all who have longed for his appearing. (2 Timothy 4:6–8)

In analyzing the data using grounded theory methodology, Dr. Clinton and his team identified four overarching observations fraught with huge implications for leadership and how leadership is effectively developed.

1. Few leaders finish well.
2. Leadership is difficult.
3. God's enabling presence is the essential ingredient of successful leadership.
4. Spiritual leadership can make a difference.

In his own words, Dr. Clinton presents his findings in support of his conclusions in a series of articles addressing the topic of finishing well.[57]

---

[57] Two different versions using these three articles have been given as plenary talks at conferences. The Mantle of the Mentor (1993) by Dr. J. Robert Clinton was given at a plenary address spoken at the International Foursquare Convention in Lexington, Kentucky. Emphasizes finishing well. Three case studies set the stage for the presentation of six barriers to finishing well and five enhancements to finishing well. Few leaders finish well. The thrust of this address is to warn and motivate many more to finish well. Finishing Well (1994) by Dr. J. Robert Clinton. A second plenary address was spoken at the Leadership Forum Conference at Estes Park, CO, sponsored by Interest Ministries of Wheaton, IL. Four case studies set the stage for presentation of six barriers to finishing well and five enhancements to finishing well. The thrust of this address was to warn

Identifying the fact that few leaders finish well was a breakthrough warning for me. This led to further study. Why do few leaders finish well? What stops them? What helps them? What does it mean to finish well? Comparative study of effective leaders who finished well has identified *six characteristics*. While there may be other characteristics that I have not seen, certainly these are important ones. Not all six always appear but at least several of them do in leaders who finish well. Frequently, effective leaders who finish well will have four or five of them seen in their lives. And some like Daniel in the O.T. and Paul in the N.T. demonstrate all of them.[58]

I cannot imagine a follower of Christ who does not want to finish well. How we cross the finish line matters. How we start is less important than how we finish. What does a person who finished well look like? What observable characteristics are evident in his/her life? What does the person's life journey indicate? To what does he/she aspire? What is the focus of his/her life?

When the lives of biblical, historical, and contemporary Christian leaders were examined, and case studies were completed, six characteristics of leaders who finished well emerged. Not all leaders studied possessed all the characteristics, but most had two or more dominant traits. Although undoubtedly incomplete, the following qualities emerged repeatedly:

- Spiritually vibrant: one who maintained a personal, vibrant relationship with God right up to the end
- Learner: one who maintained a learning posture and continually learns from various kinds of sources, life in particular

---

and motivate many more to finish well. These two Finishing Well talks can be ordered from the purchase section of this website as TwoFinishingWellTalks.pdf.

[58] J. Robert Clinton. "Finishing Well—Six Characteristics," *ScribD*, 2007. https://www.scribd.com/document/108953759/Finishing-Well-Six-Characteristics.

- Christlike: one who gave evidence of Christlikeness in character, as seen by the fruit of the Spirit in a life.
- Faithful and obedient: one who lived out truth in a lie so that convictions and promises of God are seen to be real
- Legacy: one who left behind one or more ultimate contributions; that is, a lasting legacy.

Those who were cut off early, finished so-so or poorly, and didn't finish well encountered barriers they were unable to get through. These barriers still prevent believers from finishing well today.

Some time ago I approached my boss, suggesting that my business card be changed. Somewhat bemused, he said it couldn't get much longer. I said I wanted to shorten it to a title that reflected the primary role of a leader of others—barrier remover. Our job as leaders of others is to remove any impediment that restricts them from performing at their optimum best. Our job is to help them flourish from the foundation of their wiring; to be all God intended them to be and to realize their full potential. In doing so, the organizations they serve will benefit.

There are barriers, however, that are self-inflicted. If these barriers are not addressed, they will prevent a leader from finishing well. To be sure, each barrier has gradations or degrees of dysfunctionality. The degree to which a barrier impedes a leader will determine the degree to which his/her effectiveness is limited and thus his/her hope of finishing well. J. Robert Clinton identified six barriers to finishing well.[59] Others could be added for sure, but these six dominated the research:

- Finances: their use and abuse (Gideon's golden ephod, Ananias and Sapphira)
- Power: its abuse (Uzziah's usurping of priestly privilege)
- Inordinate pride: leading to a downfall (David's numbering)
- Sex: illicit relationships (David and Bathsheba)

---

[59] Paul Leavenworth and Richard Clinton. *Starting Well: Building a Strong Foundation for a Lifetime of Ministry* (Altadena: Barnabas Publishers, 1998), 17–19.

- Family: critical (unresolved) issues (David's family, Ammon and Tamar, Absalom)
- Plateauing: living off fumes (David, latter part of reign before son's revolt)
- Emotional and psychological wounding: scarred by people, circumstances, or events (Cain, Esau, Absalom, Judas)

Given these findings, what practices will help us finish well?[60]

- Perspective: a broad perspective on a lifetime of ministry from which to interpret ongoing ministry.
- Renewal: expectancy for renewal. All leaders should expectantly look for repeated times of renewal.
- Disciplines: the practice of disciplines. Leaders need discipline of all kinds.
- Learning posture: the single most important antidote for plateauing is a well-developed learning posture.
- Mentors: Leaders who finish well have had anywhere from ten to fifteen significant mentors in their lives.

QUESTIONS TO PONDER

If you keep going as you are, what legacy will you leave?
What needs to change to finish well?
Which of these characteristics are true of you?
What do you desire your legacy to be?

RECOMMENDED RESOURCE

Finishing Well: Establishing a Lasting Legacy, volume 3 (2012) by Dr. Richard Clinton and Dr. Paul Leavenworth

---

[60] Paul Leavenworth and Richard Clinton. *Starting Well: Building a Strong Foundation for a Lifetime of Ministry* (Altadena: Barnabas Publishers, 1998), 19–24.

READING (ABSORBING WHAT MATTERS)

Of making many books there is no end, and
much study wearies the body.
—Ecclesiastes 12:12

Have you ever felt there is not enough time in the day to read what needs to be read? Emails, postings, articles, studies, and books clamor for our attention. How can a leader possibly expect to stay abreast of the hurricane of information relevant to his/her calling or profession? Leaders need to be able to sort through vast amounts of written materials to stay abreast of their occupational fields.

My mentor, J. Robert Clinton, introduced me to *continuum reading concepts*. He proposes that continuum reading is

> Useful to direct a reader to process vast amounts of information at some level of acquisition and lesser amounts at more in depth levels of acquisition and evaluation, with an ultimate view of identifying and using concepts in one's own leadership… Most people learn to read by reading every word on every page. The Reading Continuum assumes that one does not have to read every word to benefit from the information. One can read different books differently and obtain useful

information without having to read every word of every book.[61]

The Reading Continuum

Scan	Ransack	Browse	Pre-Read	In Depth Read	Study
Overview contents	New ideas; specific ideas	Some in-depth contextual analysis	Determine thematic intent; structural intent	Analysis of thematic intent; evaluation analysis	Repeated work in the book; comparative analysis

Assessment Levels	Evaluation Levels

Many Books	Few Books

The ability to read various kinds of books differently is a valuable skill and almost a necessity for anyone involved in leadership and leadership training, since so much has been written on the subject.

Dr. Clinton describes the relationship between the levels. *Study*, at the right is the most in-depth level of reading. At the left is the lightest kind of reading, called *scan*. In between are various kinds of reading, each increasing in terms of depth, intensity, time invested, and amount covered as one moves to the right. Clinton goes on to say each level to the right includes the various features involved in all reading levels to the left. The ability to read various kinds of books differently is a valuable skill and almost a necessity for anyone involved in leadership and leadership training.

Dr. Clinton states that the reading continuum is not related to speed-reading skills. Speed-reading programs teach one how to rapidly scan words. A person can be a very fast or very slow reader and still use continuum reading concepts. These concepts teach one how to pick and choose which words, paragraphs, pages, chapters, and sections should be read and how to read them for information without having to read every word.

---

[61]   J. Robert Clinton. *Reading on the Run, Continuum Reading Concepts* (Pasadena: Barnabas Publishers, 1999), 1–3.

Not every word of every book or article requires reading. What you read and how much you read depends on the material being read. As J. Robert Clinton declared,

> One can read different books *(articles)* differently and obtain useful information without having to read every word of every book *(article)*. Continuum reading concepts teach one how to pick and choose which words, paragraphs, pages, chapters and sections are to be read, and how to read them for information without having to read every word.[62]

Six levels of reading intensity are proposed: scan, ransack, browse, pre-read, in-depth reading, and study. The remarks that follow come directly from *Reading on the Run: Continuum Reading Concepts* by J. Robert Clinton (Barnabas Publishers, 1999).

SCAN READING

Scan reading allows one to survey the potential value of reading a book without committing too much time to it. It is the initial approach to reading a book.

Scan reading is an overview approach to reading a book. This involves a careful reading of the table of contents, introductory information, and dust-cover remarks, along with any information on the author that will allow at least a cursory understanding of what the book is about and how it is organized, with a view toward determining what further level along the continuum the book should be read.

Scanning also includes thumbing through the book to note any conclusions, summary statements, charts, tables, possibility of useful quotes, illustrations, and so on. Some books can be scanned in as little as fifteen minutes. Some books may take as much as two hours.

---

[62] Ibid., 3.

SIX RESULTS FROM SCAN READING

When you have scanned a book, you will know who wrote the book, will have identified the author's perspective, will know how the book is organized, will recognize what the author is trying to accomplish, will have identified further assessment reading possibilities (ransacking/browsing), and will have made a decision concerning evaluative reading—whether to do (e.g., will do now, will do in future, will not do), decide after ransacking or browsing, which level to do [preread, in-depth read, or study]).

RANSACK READING

When you are relatively familiar with certain topics, you may not need to read every chapter in a book but may choose to read very selectively. That is, you may read given portions to see if they add any new ideas or ideas different from those of which you are already aware.

Close ransacking refers to reading while only looking for a preselected topic of interest. It refers to rapid reading to compare or contrast what is said with some already known idea or ideas in mind.

Open ransacking refers to reading while looking for new ideas. It refers to rapid reading to see if there is some new idea or new slant on an idea concerning some specific area of interest.

Ransack reading refers to the technique of looking through a book to see what it says concerning a specific topic of interest or combing through a book on relatively familiar material to see if it has any new ideas not known to you.

SIX RESULTS FROM RANSACK READING

When you have ransacked a book, you will have noted a new idea on a preselected topic of interest to you, noted a contrasting or differing idea on some preselected topic of interest to you, determined that the book has nothing to add to your preselected topic of interest, gained something worth noting that is of interest to you on any topic, determined that nothing of interest to you can be gained from the book, made a tentative decision concerning pre-read, in-depth reading, or study (e.g., will do now, will do in future, not necessary to do, decide after ransacking or browsing).

BROWSE READING

Browsing is dipping into certain portions of a book to study in detail some discussion of a topic in its contextual treatment. Having scanned a book, you may decide that you are relatively familiar with the material and want to explore in some detail a given topic of interest. Detailed reading of an extended portion (or portions) of a book is what is meant by browsing. Often you will discover browsing material when ransacking for a new idea (concept, strategy, process, principle, methodology, etc.).

FIVE RESULTS FROM BROWSE READING

When browsing, prepare evaluation-type questions on a limited portion of the book you are reading, organized around the concept, strategy, process, principle, methodology, etc. you are seeking to explore. The following questions are helpful to browsing.

- What did the author say on the subject of interest? Resist initially reading into what the author is saying.
- How well did the author say it? What definitions, examples, figures of speech, cogency of argument, or substantiation was employed?
- What did the author leave unsaid? What lingering questions remain in the mind of the reader that should have been addressed?
- How do the author's words compare to what you have read or learned elsewhere? How does the material differ or contrast with what has been said elsewhere?
- How useful is the information? What new insights are gained? What new perspective has been achieved? How will what has been learned be operationalized?

PREREADING

Prereading a book is a special kind of survey of a book that involves drawing implications from various portions of the book as to the thematic and structural intent of the book. Prereading a book indicates a serious intent to understand an entire book. When you pre-read a book, you are seeking to find out the overall thematic content of the book and to see how the author has structured the material to develop the thematic intent.

Structural intent refers to a recognition of how the author uses each portion of the book to contribute to the subject or major ideas of the book. Thematic intent refers to a single statement that weaves together the main subject of the book and each major idea developed throughout the book.

You pre-read a book when, in your scanning, ransacking, and browsing, you determine that the book is well written and has developed an important topic in an organized manner. In prereading a book, you will do your best to identify a single statement of what the author is saying without reading the entire book. It is a special kind of survey that requires careful thinking and extrapolation, based on a limited amount of information.

The skills to do this are developed only with practice. After you have pre-read several books and then have followed with reading (the entire book) and discovered how well your prereading agrees or disagrees with your reading, you will develop skill and confidence in your ability to pre-read.

FOUR RESULTS FROM PREREADING

When you have pre-read a book, you will have tentative statements describing the kind of book that was pre-read; the author's intent and methodology; the author's thesis, which involves the major subject and supporting major ideas; and the intent of each major section (or minor, where necessary) and how they contribute to the thesis statement.

IN-DEPTH READING

According to J. Robert Clinton (and in his own words), you do an in-depth reading of a book when you have determined from scanning, ransacking, and browsing that it is worth prereading and reading in depth. An in-depth reading of a book is a detailed approach to the evaluation of a book, which involves prereading followed by detailed reading of all parts of the text to affirm, deny, or modify the prereading analysis and to produce six evaluation statements.

Reading a book is a serious, detailed approach to the understanding of what the author is saying. It is an approach that says the book deserves to be read in a detailed enough way that you can give evaluation statements about the book as a whole. When you have read a book, you have an overall grasp of the book and can discuss it motivationally with a potential reader. You will be able to discuss six kinds of evaluation statements, which are described below.

SIX RESULTS FROM IN-DEPTH READING

You will have revealed, if appropriate, the following information:

1. Shown where the author is uninformed in his/her writing (e.g., examples from the book where the author draws conclusions without considering all the facts)
2. Shown where the author is misinformed in his/her writing, (e.g., instances/examples from the book in which the author draws conclusions based on false information)
3. Shown where the author is illogical in his/her writing (e.g., examples from the book in which the author uses faulty reasoning in arriving at conclusions)
4. Shown where the author's analysis or account is incomplete in terms of his/her statement of purpose in writing the book (e.g., an evaluation of the author's accomplishment of purpose in writing the book)
5. Shown the author's strengths in his/her writing (e.g., reference to useful quotations, point out any strong arguments or

explanations, and point out concepts that can be transferred to your own experience)

6. Shown the relevance of the book to today's needs (e.g., application to various life situations to which the book can be applied. You can point out the kind of reader who will profit the most by the book)

STUDYING A BOOK

Studying a book requires the most detailed kind of reading. Studying a book is a special in-depth approach to the reading of a book that involves prereading, reading, and background research on materials and ideas used in the book. It involves the ability to do comparative evaluation and original research on materials and ideas used in the book.

SIX RESULTS FROM STUDYING A BOOK

When you have studied a book, you will accomplish the following:

1. Do the four prereading statements.
2. Arrive at appropriate evaluation statements from the six evaluation statements normally considered in detailed reading.
3. Be able to discuss the book analytically with another reader.
4. Be able to evaluate the other reader's analysis for clarification, modification, etc.
5. Research original materials quoted in the book for evaluating accuracy.
6. Compare the book with other books dealing with the same major subject to show similarities, differences, unique contributions, etc.

I hope the information on continuum reading concepts will inform your reading practices going forward. I strongly recommend you acquire this handy guide by purchasing *Reading on the Run: Continuum Reading Concepts* by J. Robert Clinton (1987). There is much more detail, including examples of each reading method and feedback on each method. There is also information in this valuable resource for writing a book review using reading continuum concepts.

QUESTIONS TO PONDER

How do you read a book?

What level of reading intensity is warranted for the books in your possession?

How will your reading change because of these concepts?

RECOMMENDED RESOURCE

Reading on the Run, Continuum Reading Concepts (1999) by Dr. J. Robert Clinton

HEART

CALLING (DETERMINING YOUR DESTINY)

Calling is a confusing concept for ministry leaders and followers of Jesus Christ. Does God *call* a person to a specific role, a specific location, a specific church, or a specific ministry organization? To be sure, God can do whatever he wants. He can certainly call us to any role, location, church, or organization. As believers, we are all called to ministry, not just those who are called to the vocation of professional ministry.

But often we are free to choose any of these within God's permissive will, based on the purpose and function he ordained for us before we ever came to be. If it doesn't violate his commands or moral law, we are free to choose.

We are called to serve the purpose and function he designed for each of us specifically.

First, we are called according to his design.

Second, we are called to serve a function rather than a role. Our function includes spiritual gift(s), natural abilities, acquired skills, personality temperament, leadership style, values, and ministry principles—collectively, they represent the function we are to serve, rather than the place, location, or role we might embrace.

Third, God may open multiple avenues, options, or opportunities, where the full expression of our designed function can be exercised. This certainly would include a consideration of a place, location, or role.

Fourth, under the umbrella of God's permissive will, we are free to choose the avenue, option, or opportunity that will provide the context where our purpose and function can flourish.

Fifth, God calls us to properly steward our designed function. Again, God can do whatever he wants and can call us directly to a role, a location, or a church, for that matter. But in my humble opinion, this is an exception to the rule. The rule I speak of is that God calls us to serve the purpose and function for which he has designed us.

In 1 Corinthians 12:4–7, we have what I call the gift package. "There are different kinds of gifts, but the same Spirit. There are different kinds of service, but the same Lord. There are different kinds of working, but the same God works all of them in all men. Now to each one the manifestation of the Spirit is given for the common good."

Notice first that the Trinity is involved (*Spirit*, Jesus our *Lord*, and *God* the Father).

Second, to each of us has been given a "manifestation of the Spirit for the common good."

In 1 Peter 4:10, we read that "each one should use whatever gift he has received to serve others, faithfully administering God's grace in its various forms." Third, there are different kinds of gifts, different kinds of service, and different kinds of working. Gifts, service, and workings comprise what I call the gift package.

- There are different *gifts*. The list of possible gifts can be found in three places.[63] Each believer is given one or more gifts at the moment of conversion to help the body of Christ become more like Christ in our thoughts, words, and deeds.
- There are different kinds of *service* in which the gifts can be expressed. This could include avenues of expression, such as roles or occupations, settings, or contexts, such as churches, location, or ministry organizations.
- There are different kinds of *working*. When individuals are faithful in the expression of their gifts in the avenues the Lord provides for such expression, they will enjoy a measure of

---

[63] 1 Corinthians 12:8–10; Ephesians 4:7–13; Romans 12:3–8.

godly effectiveness as they seek to serve the Lord faithfully in accordance with their gifts and the opportunities he offers them.

Let's look at the possibilities.

Calling	Occupation	Setting
Function	Role	Area
Giftedness/Wiring	*Profession/Career*	*Location/Site*
Missionary	Church Planter	City/County
Shepherd	Senior Pastor	Church
Family	Parent	Home
Benefactor	Business Person	Company
Leader	Ministry Director	Parachurch
Leader	Small Group Leader	Church
Teacher	Graduate Education	Seminary
Shepherd	Associate Pastor	Church
Evangelist	Children's Pastor	Country
Teacher	Secondary Education	High School
Leader	Trustee	Church Board
Shepherd	Single's Pastor	Church
Administrator	Business Manager	Ministry Agency
Prophet	Preacher	At Large
Evangelist	Preacher	Street
Teacher	Sunday School Teacher	Church
Leader	Senator	Government
Mentor	Business Person	Organization
Your Wiring	Your Chosen Field	Your Chosen Setting

Notice, for instance, that the spiritual gift of teaching might find its full expression in graduate education at a seminary or as a Sunday school teacher in a church. Likewise, the gift of leadership might find its full expression as a ministry director in a parachurch ministry organization, as a small-group leader in a church, as a trustee on a church board, or as a senior pastor of a church.

More succinctly, God calls us to ministry in direct correlation with our servant's profile—spiritual gifting, talent, temperament, passion, spiritual maturity (our wiring). He may lead us to a particular location or expression of our calling. In the former, he is the initiator; in the latter, he is our partner.

Ben Patterson, in his book *Serving God* (1994),[64] draws a distinction between vocation and occupation. He says the word vocation should refer to our *calling*. Occupation, on the other hand, refers to our work. Christians can have many different occupations, but just one vocation. In other words, we are called to one vocation, which can be expressed in many occupations or locations. He further makes a subtle distinction between calling (vocation) and many callings (occupations).

According to *Nelson's Bible Dictionary*,[65] vocation is a call or an invitation to a profession or way of life. But in theological discussions, the word *vocation* is not used in reference to the professional trade one pursues. Vocation refers to the invitation God has given to all people to become his children through Christ's work. This vocation, or calling, does not come to people because they deserve it; it comes strictly because of God's grace.[66] However, it is up to the individual to decide whether he/she will accept and act upon the vocation.

The framework suggested above is applicable to spiritual gifts.

> There are different kinds of gifts, but the same Spirit.
> There are different kinds of service, but the same Lord.
> There are different kinds of working, but the same God
> works all of them in all men. Now to each one the

---

[64] Ben Patterson, *Serving God: The Grand Essentials of Work and Worship* (Downers Grove: Intervarsity Press, 1994).

[65] Ronald F. Youngblood (author), F. F. Bruce (contributor), R. K. Harrison (contributor), *Nelson's Illustrated Bible Dictionary: New and Enhanced Edition* (Nashville: Thomas Nelson Publishers, 2014).

[66] 2 Timothy 1:9.

manifestation of the Spirit is given for the common good. (1 Corinthians 12:4–7)

We may have one or more gifts; that doesn't change, but how these gifts are expressed and the effectiveness we enjoy in the expression of those gifts varies.

Gary Friesen, in his book *Decision Making and the Will of God* (2004),[67] proposes that under God's permissive will we have the freedom to choose alternatives without the fear of missing the dot in God's will. Unless God intervenes, or the Word of God gives clear direction, we are free to choose from many possible alternatives. He calls this the *way of wisdom*. Four principles are espoused.

1. In those areas specifically addressed by the Bible, the revealed commands and principles of God (his moral will) are to be obeyed.
2. In those areas where the Bible gives no command or principle (nonmoral decisions), the believer is free and responsible to choose his/her own course of action. Any decision made within the moral will of God is acceptable to God.
3. In nonmoral decisions, the objective of the Christian is to make wise decisions based on spiritual expediency.
4. In all decisions, the believer should humbly submit, in advance, to the outworking of God's sovereign will as it touches each decision.

In summary, we are called (or set apart) for the ministry of the gospel—our vocation. Second, we express our calling in one or more callings (occupations). Third, we may be led to a particular situation (setting). Our calling is initiated by God. Our calling (or callings) is our response to his gifting, and we may be led to a particular situation (setting). In the last scenario, we are free to choose, without fear of

---

[67] Garry Friesen, *Decision Making and the Will of God: A Biblical Alternative to the Traditional View* (Sisters: Multnomah Press, 2004), 116.

penalty, for "all things work together for good to those who love God and are called according to his purpose."[68]

QUESTIONS TO PONDER

What are your spiritual gifts, natural abilities, and acquired skills (giftedness)?

How are you leveraging your giftedness to facilitate God's redemptive purposes?

How can you express how God has wired you?

RECOMMENDED RESOURCE

Serving God: The Essentials of Work and Worship (1994) by Ben Patterson

---

[68] Romans 8:28.

VALUES (IDENTIFYING THE PRINCIPLES YOU WILL LIVE BY)

A leader's beliefs and values will affect his/her judgment and behavior, regardless of protestations otherwise!

Hopeful politicians showcase their wares in anticipation of being elected to office. Amid the blather we are subjected to on news channels with growing frequency, we hear a common pronouncement of the values they hold. Much of the rhetoric seeks to create a bond with the voters by suggesting that the politician identifies with and shares common values with the masses, whom he or she hopes will elect him or her over other candidates.

Just because a person declares a value set like your own, you cannot assume he or she is the same as you. For instance, let's say the candidate espouses a value for family. Sounds good, but what does the person really mean? Or let's say a leader stresses the value of integrity. We may think we know what is meant, but we can't be sure. The term used to express a value may the same, but the expression and outcome may be entirely opposite to our expectations. Why is that?

When a person says that he will suspend his personal beliefs or values to govern effectively, he portrays an impossible scenario. No matter how hard she tries, she cannot divorce herself from her inner convictions and beliefs. They can mask them, they can hide them, they can try to suspend them, but they will not be able to remove their influence. What we truly believe (trust in, rely on, cling to) establishes our values (what we esteem). Our beliefs and values are a fundamental part of our intellectual, emotional, and spiritual makeup and wiring.

Simply declaring a value is not significant, in and of itself. Declaring what gives rise to and influences our values is significant. We can envision the behavior produced by a declared value when we consider what gives life to that value for the one expressing it.

I have yet to hear a journalist press politicians to explain what they mean about a value they say they hold. More significantly, I have yet to hear a reporter ask a variation of the following question: What informs, conditions, and establishes the values you say you hold?

In the spirit of full disclosure, I have personally chosen Jesus Christ and the Bible to be my authority for faith and practice. When I allow something else to creep in and unseat this authority, the decisions I make, and the behavior produced is inconsistent with what I say I believe. Competing authorities will always be there. I must decide what will rule my beliefs, values, and behavior daily.

In its simplest form, values are the hills you are prepared to die on, the principles you intend to live by, and the filter through which decisions are processed and made. Every decision we have made, are making, or will make is based on the values we hold, whether or not we can articulate them.

For many of us, our system of values is an unordered set of qualities often in conflict with one another. One day, we make a decision of merit; the next day, a bad decision with negative consequences. For still others, the consistency of the decisions they make may indicate a congruent system of values.

Like beliefs, values can be aspirations rather than observable realities in our lives. Men and women often ask me to mentor them. They know I am big on values, so they often begin their comments by stating their values. I listen intently and respectfully. I then ask them the following question: What decision have you made or what action have you taken within the last three months that gives evidence of the values you say you hold? Many of them cannot give me any examples. This is because the values they say they hold may simply be an interest, preference, or affirmation but not an actionable commitment yet.

The most important question to ask, however, is what stands in the privileged vantage point of authority over your values? Whatever stands in a position of authority over one's value system will determine the quality and substance of the behavior it produces.

For instance, a Christian can have a value for truth—and so can a humanist or atheist. What that value produces in one person's behaviors will more than likely be different from the others. A Christian's underlying belief may be that Jesus is the way, the truth, and the life, and if he holds to Jesus's teaching, he will know the truth, and the truth will set him free. His behavior has the focus of living by God's truth, instead of the world's truth. For the humanist, having a value for truth may be favorable for business or the esteem of respected colleagues. The practice of truth for the atheist may be to promote his or her beliefs as the only truth. You see, what informs your values makes all the difference.

When values are loosely acquired without attention to any ordering structure or congruent belief system, the values can produce conflictive results—they may be inconsistent from one day to the next, depending on the circumstance or the situation.

Many authorities compete for influence over our values, including tradition, heritage, experience, convention, culture, some ideology or philosophy, our faith, or some *-ism*, such as postmodernism, Marxism, capitalism, socialism, humanism, or a combination of some or all of them.

Some of us are unclear about our values. Answers to the following questions might clarify your values:

- What is it that I treasure so highly that I am irritated when other people don't also treasure it?
- What are the things I respect so deeply that I tend to be resentful of those who treat them with disrespect?
- If I knew that I had six months to live, what would become the most important to me?
- What would become unimportant to me?
- What core value(s) do I hope my children will adopt?

If it were possible to follow you around without being noticed for the next three months, I would be able to tell you what you truly valued. Your behavior, over time, would reveal your values. If I could talk to people close to you—a wife or a husband, a brother or a sister, a father or a mother, or a close friend—and I asked them what your values are, they could probably tell me. If I were to ask your work associates what you valued, they could probably tell me.

I often give an exercise to the people I mentor. I instruct them to meet with their spouses or loved ones or someone who really knows them. They are to assure that person that there will be no argument with or consequences to his or her response when they ask this person the following question: Based on your observations of my behaviors over time, what would you say are my values?

Acting on your values over an extended period will embed them in your spiritual DNA. When that happens, they cease to be a value to be cultivated and become a virtue that marks your character. You operate from them without much thought because they are now an integral part of who you are.

What informs, conditions, mediates, and establishes your value set will determine the nature, quality, and substance of the behavior it produces.

QUESTIONS TO PONDER

Are your values an aspiration or an operational commitment?

What informs and conditions the values you say you hold?

What provides consistency, coherence, and congruence to your value system?

What organizes and prioritizes your values?

What would your loved ones, work associates, friends (and enemies) say you value?

How do the values you say you hold inform what you do?

RECOMMENDED RESOURCE

Winning the Values War in a Changing Culture: Thirteen Distinct Values That Mark a Follower of Jesus Christ (1994) by Leith Anderson

INTEGRITY (LIVING A LIFE OF CONGRUITY)

Integrity is all about character; it is about your core values that ultimately shape your life—it is about having a consistency of character that matches your words, actions, choices, values, and behaviors.

AN INCONVENIENT MOMENT

I was leading a group of men in three separate groups through a journey called the Map. We put our personal timelines together as the first step in developing our personal life mandates. In doing so, we looked at the process items God uses to shape us into the image of Christ. One such process item is called an integrity check—a test God uses to evaluate the heart and consistency of inner convictions with outward actions.

Integrity checks come by way of temptation, conflict, persecution, values check, or challenge to follow through on some commitment made earlier. It's not that God doesn't know how we'll respond. We must know how we'll respond. God allows such checks to firm up our spiritual backbones. Sometimes we fail. Other times we pass the test. In either case we learn something about ourselves.

Not too long ago, I received such a check. I went to the grocery store to pick up several items, including two pounds of coffee. When I got home I looked at my receipt. The coffee was nowhere on it. Here is what went through my mind:

- I have been cheated in the past; this makes up for it.
- I'm really tired, and I don't want to get in the car and go all the way back to the store.
- I'll purchase two pounds of coffee at another time, and give it away.
- Maybe this is God's gift to me.

None of these excuses were enough to overcome the internal conviction of the Holy Spirit, but it was close. Because I am a follower of Christ, and because I have trained hundreds of men to live lives of integrity and honor under God's authority, and because I had just told the men in our groups about integrity checks, I knew what I had to do. I got in my car, drove back to the store with the coffee, and stood in the checkout lane, waiting for my turn. When I got to the cashier, I said, "This might sound a little strange but …" Then I told him what had happened. He looked at me, surprised, rang up the coffee, and then told me he had given me a 30 percent discount because of my honesty. I told him it wasn't necessary.

Why do I share this with you?

I normally keep such things to myself, but since I had just taught men the importance of integrity check, I thought it might be instructive for others. The journey to becoming a man after God's heart never ends. We must be prepared for the challenges that shape our characters and our destiny. I can certainly recount those that I failed. By the grace of God, I want to be a man of integrity. I hope you do too.

In scripture we read, "Whoever can be trusted with very little can also be trusted with much, and whoever is dishonest with very little will also be dishonest with much. So, if you have not been trustworthy in handling worldly wealth, who will trust you with true riches? And if you have not been trustworthy with someone else's property, who will give you property of your own?"[69] Faithfulness begins with small things.

When I got home the second time, I realized that I had left a twelve-pack of cream soda under the basket of my cart the first time I was at the store. It wasn't in my trunk. I had forgotten to take it out of the cart and put it in my trunk. I had to laugh. Go figure.

INTEGRITY DEFINED

The dictionary defines *integrity* as a firm adherence to a code of especially moral or artistic values, or incorruptibility; incapable of being bribed or morally corrupted. Integrity is described as soundness of moral character.

Integrity, from a biblical perspective, suggests being morally sound. In the Bible, the Hebrew word translated as integrity in the Old Testament means the condition of being without blemish, completeness, perfection, sincerity, soundness, uprightness, wholeness.

Integrity in the New Testament means honesty and adherence to a pattern of good works.

Jesus is the perfect example of a man of integrity. After he was baptized, he went into the wilderness to fast for forty days and nights, during which time Satan came to him at his weakest to try to break his integrity and corrupt him. Jesus was wholly man and wholly God at the same time, and he was tempted in every way we are, yet he never sinned;[70] that is the definition of integrity. He is the only one who was ever without blemish, perfect, completely truthful, and always showed a pattern of good works. As sinful human beings, our integrity is flawed, but Jesus's integrity is perfect. When we are "in Christ," we partake of his divine nature, having been given new natures in Christ (2 Corinthians 5:17), and that new nature is one of integrity because it is his nature.

John Maxwell defines integrity this way:

---

[69] Luke 16:10–12.
[70] Hebrews 4:14.

Integrity binds our person together and fosters a spirit of contentment within us. It will not allow our lips to violate our hearts. When integrity is the referee, we will be consistent; our beliefs will be mirrored by our conduct. There will be no discrepancy between what we appear to be and what our family knows we are, whether in times of prosperity or adversity. Integrity allows us to predetermine what we will be regardless of circumstances, persons involved, or the places of our testing.[71]

"Let your yes be yes, and your no be no."[72]

INTEGRITY EXPLAINED

Integrity has been called the key to character and the cure for inconsistency. In scripture, we read the following: "Remember your leaders, who spoke the word of God to you. Consider the outcome of their way of life and imitate their faith. Jesus Christ is the same yesterday and today and forever."[73]

First, integrity is better caught than taught. Notice that we are to remember our leaders, consider the outcome of their lives, and imitate their faith. The next verse seems to drop in out of nowhere and seems out of place with the preceding verse. Closer scrutiny, however, reveals the character trait that is true of leaders who are worth following—consistency.

Our model for integrity, Jesus Christ, was the same yesterday, today, and forever. Integrity worth emulating is consistently demonstrated over time. In other words, a man or woman of integrity shows consistency—a uniformity, reliability, steadiness, constancy, and stability in their

---

71 John C. Maxwell, *Maxwell Daily Reader: 365 Days of Insight to Develop the Leader Within You and Influence Those Around You* (Nashville: Thomas Nelson, 2007), 262.

72 Matthew 5:37.

73 Hebrews 13:7–8.

character, their decisions, and their behavior. The pattern of their lives shows an evenness in how they live their lives.

In other words, integrity has to do with a sense of consistency between a person's inner values and attitudes and his or her outward words and actions. The more consistent we are, the higher the degree of integrity we possess. A good biblical example of integrity is Daniel.[74]

Daniel's values, words, and actions were thoroughly consistent. You can't put a price tag on integrity because genuine integrity is not for sale. Integrity helps us know what to expect from others. The more consistent people are, the more confidence we have in how they will act in the future. Unpredictable leaders suggest that they are not making decisions based on deeply held biblical values but on how they may feel now. It is hard, if not impossible, to trust such people. People will trust those who have proved themselves to be trustworthy.

A lack of integrity is marked by a pattern of inconsistency—inconsistency between what a person says and what he or she does; inconsistency between one's proclaimed values and the decisions one makes; inconsistency in the actions taken over time.

Second, integrity can be observed and recognized. Psalm 15 describes eleven behavioral characteristics of integrity.[75]

Lord, who may dwell in your sanctuary? Who may live on your holy hill?

1. He whose walk is blameless (irreproachable),
2. And who does what is righteous (honorable),
3. Who speaks the truth from his heart,
4. And has no slander (defamation) on his tongue,
5. Who does his neighbor no wrong,
6. And casts no slur (insult) on his fellowman,
7. Who despises a vile (despicable and abhorrent) man,
8. But honors those who fear the Lord,
9. Who keeps his oath, even when it hurts,

---

[74] Daniel 5:13–17.
[75] Psalm 15:1–5.

10. Who lends his money without usury (exorbitant interest),

11. And does not accept a bribe against the innocent.

He who does these things will never be shaken.

Third, integrity produces to authenticity. I define an authentic Christian as one who conforms to the original, Jesus Christ, and reproduces those features that reflect his character. Such individuals leave little doubt to whom they belong because they bear the imprint of the Master.

To be authentic means to be true, reliable, dependable, faithful, trustworthy, and genuine. Being a man or woman of integrity means you are the same in the dark as you are in the light. Being a man or woman of authenticity means you are that same way all the time.

Integrity brings soundness of character with adherence to good moral principles; for instance, uprightness and honesty.

Fourth, integrity can be measured. Honest answers to the following questions posed by an author about integrity can reveal the degree to which integrity is present in our lives.

- What are you like when no one else is around?
- How do you treat others who can't benefit you?
- How sincere, humble, and transparent are you?
- Are you the same person when you are with different people?
- Are you the same person in public as in private?
- Do you quickly admit to yourself and others when you're wrong?
- Do you subscribe to God's absolute moral standards in his Word?
- Do you talk to people or about them behind their backs?
- Are you accountable to at least one person for what you think, say, and do?
- Do you submit to God's Spirit and seek to please him in all you do?

One writer put it succinctly. To walk in integrity is to reveal a habitual manner of life. Integrity is 100 percent lifestyle.

INTEGRITY DEVELOPED

How does one develop and nurture integrity? Integrity can be cultivated. The practice of integrity is a daily decision we make. Being a person of integrity requires dependence on God, focused living, proactive intentionality, self-discipline, and dedication. You must want to be a person of integrity to become of person of integrity.

1. Choose to become a person of integrity.
2. Use biblical beliefs and values to shape and establish your integrity.
3. Be accountable to someone for your integrity.
4. Recognize and positively respond to integrity checks.
5. Be honest with yourself and others when you are not a person of integrity.
6. Seek out a godly mentor who models integrity.
7. Keep your promises; don't make promises you can't keep.
8. Commit to cultivating honesty, reliability, and consistency.
9. Decide in advance to do the right thing, no matter what.
10. Don't give up, no matter how many times you fail.

Other scripture underscores the importance of integrity.

"As for you, if you walk before me in integrity of heart and uprightness, as David your father did, and do all I command and observe my decrees and laws" (1 Kings 9:4–5).

"I know, my God, that you test the heart and are pleased with integrity" (1 Chronicles 29:17).

"He does not oppress anyone but returns what he took in pledge for a loan. He does not commit robbery but gives his food to the hungry and provides clothing for the naked. He does not lend at usury or take excessive interest. He withholds his hand from doing wrong and judges fairly between man and man. He follows my decrees and faithfully keeps my laws. That man is righteous; he will surely live, declares the Sovereign Lord" (Ezekiel 18:7–9).

"I put in charge of Jerusalem my brother Hanani, along with

Hananiah the commander of the citadel, because he was a man of integrity and feared God more than most men do" (Nehemiah 7:2–3).

"Then the Lord said to Satan, 'Have you considered my servant Job? There is no one on earth like him; he is blameless and upright, a man who fears God and shuns evil. And he still maintains his integrity, though you incited me against him to ruin him without any reason'" (Job 2:3).

"His wife said to him, 'Are you still holding on to your integrity? Curse God and die!'" (Job 2:9).

"My lips will not speak wickedness, and my tongue will utter no deceit. I will never admit you are in the right; till I die, I will not deny my integrity. I will maintain my righteousness and never let go of it; my conscience will not reproach me as long as I live" (Job 27:4–6).

"Let the Lord judge the peoples. Judge me, O Lord, according to my righteousness, according to my integrity, O Most High" (Psalm 7:8).

"In my integrity you uphold me and set me in your presence forever" (Psalm 41:12).

"And David shepherded them with integrity of heart; with skillful hands, he led them" (Psalm 78:72).

"The man of integrity walks securely, but he who takes crooked paths will be found out … The integrity of the upright guides them, but the unfaithful are destroyed by their duplicity" (Proverbs 10:9; 11:3).

"Righteousness guards the man of integrity, but wickedness overthrows the sinner. One man pretends to be rich, yet has nothing; another pretends to be poor, yet has great wealth" (Proverbs 13:6–7).

"Bloodthirsty men hate a man of integrity and seek to kill the upright" (Proverbs 29:10).

"They sent their disciples to him along with the Herodians. 'Teacher,' they said, 'we know you are a man of integrity and that you teach the way of God in accordance with the truth. You aren't swayed by men, because you pay no attention to who they are'" (Matthew 22:16–17).

"Whoever can be trusted with very little can also be trusted with much, and whoever is dishonest with very little will also be dishonest with much. So, if you have not been trustworthy in handling worldly wealth, who will trust you with true riches? And if you have not been trustworthy with someone else's property, who will give you property of your own?" (Luke 16:10–12).

"Whatever happens, conduct yourselves in a manner worthy of the gospel of Christ. Then, whether I come and see you or only hear about you in my absence, I will know that you stand firm in one spirit, contending as one man for the faith of the gospel without being frightened in any way by those who oppose you. This is a sign to them that they will be destroyed, but that you will be saved—and that by God. For it has been granted to you on behalf of Christ not only to believe on him, but also to suffer for him, since you are going through the same struggle you saw I had, and now hear that I still have" (Philippians 1:27–30).

"In everything set them an example by doing what is good. In your teaching show integrity, seriousness and soundness of speech that cannot be condemned, so that those who oppose you may be ashamed because they have nothing bad to say about us" (Titus 2:7–8).

Are you a person of integrity? Are you a person of authenticity?

QUESTIONS TO PONDER

What integrity checks have you experienced lately, and how did you respond?

What can you do to move from inconsistency to consistency?

What must change for you to become a person of integrity?

RECOMMENDED RESOURCE

The Power of Integrity: Building a Life Without Compromise (1997) by John MacArthur

COMPASS (FINDING DIRECTION FOR YOUR LIFE)

Do you live your life by the clock or the compass? Is the frenzied activity of your life reactive or proactive? Are you in control of your schedule, or does your schedule control you? The following ancient scriptures help to frame our discussion:

> Be careful, then, how you live—not as unwise but as wise, making the most of every opportunity, because the days are evil. (Ephesians 5:15–16)

> So, teach us to number our days that we may get a heart of wisdom. (Psalm 90:12)

> Come now, you who say, "Today or tomorrow we will go into such and such a town and spend a year there and trade and make a profit"—yet you do not know what tomorrow will bring. What is your life? For you are a mist that appears for a little time and then vanishes. Instead you ought to say, "If the Lord wills, we will live and do this or that." As it is, you boast in your arrogance. All such boasting is evil. So, whoever knows

the right thing to do and fails to do it, for him it is sin. (James 4:13–17)

What problems do you have with personal time management? What percentage of time is controllable and uncontrollable? What's your biggest time-wasting activity? As you think of your team members, what are the biggest time wasters? What do you wish you had more time to do?

Steven Covey (2004) popularized a matrix depicting four types of activity.[76] Quadrants I, III, and IV are reactive activities, while quadrant II is proactive. Too much time spent in I, III, and IV results in a fast-moving, treadmill existence. Spending sufficient time in II limits and controls the effects of the other quadrant activities. Activities in this quadrant are proactive in nature.

I have adapted Covey's matrix and added other relevant activities. The R identifies the quadrant as reactive, while the P identifies the quadrant as proactive. Second, within each reactive quadrant are italicized items that represent a dysfunctional activity. The size of each quadrant, represented as equal in the depiction below, can change, depending on the percentage of activity within the quadrant. For instance, if your life is dominated by quadrant I activity, then the size of the quadrant will be much larger than the other three quadrants, thereby reducing the size and influence of the other quadrants.

---

[76] Stephen R. Covey, *The 7 Habits of Highly Effective People: Restoring the Character Ethic* (New York: Free Press, 2004), 151–154.

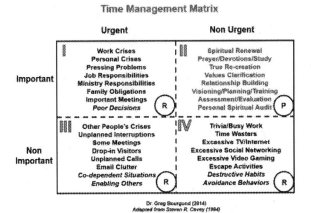

Time Management Matrix

Dr. Greg Bourgond (2014)
Adapted from Steven R. Covey (1984)

If we spend too much time in quadrant I, we are susceptible to stress, burnout, crisis management, and always putting out fires. This quadrant includes our normal responsibilities, obligations, and duties. It also includes crises of our own making, such as situations where a decision was needed but was put off. Now we have many other decisions we must make because we didn't make the critical decision initially.

Too much time spent in quadrant III results in short-term focus, crisis management, reactive leadership, little time or patience for goals and plans, feeling victimized, and feeling out of control, and it produces shallow or broken relationships. This quadrant often contains other people's crises that we assume or are triangulated in on because of their failure to complete assigned tasks we oversee.

Too much time spent in quadrant IV results in total irresponsibility, being replaced or fired from jobs, and an unhealthy dependence on others or institutions for basics. We escape to this quadrant when quadrants I and III become overwhelming. Too much time in this quadrant makes us susceptible to unhealthy activities and dysfunctional behavior.

When sufficient time is spent in quadrant II, the results are quite different: vision, perspective, centeredness, discipline, few crises, and control. Covey states, "In a successful company 20–25% of time is spent on Quadrant I activities, just 15% of time on urgent but not important (Quadrant III) activities, and 65–80% of time on Quadrant

II activities. Quadrant II activities—important but not urgent activities, are present wherever success is present."[77] Spending appropriate time in this quadrant will control the unrealistic demands or negative influence of quadrants I, III, and IV.

As indicated earlier, quadrants I, III, and IV are reactive, in that we are reacting to people, events, and circumstances. Only quadrant II is proactive. But because it is important but not urgent, we tend to put off these activities for another day, week, month, or year. Making quadrant II a high priority will, in effect, control the size and influence of quadrants I, III, and IV.

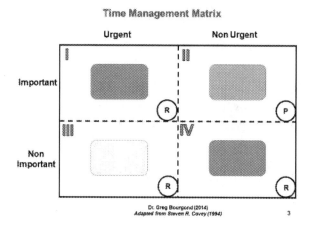

Time Management Matrix

Dr. Greg Bourgond (2014)
Adapted from Steven R. Covey (1994)   3

I strongly recommend that you conduct a personal audit of how you spend your waking moments each day. Regardless of the type of calendar you use, I suggest you track the use of your time for at least a week. I recommend the following color scheme:

For activities that fall in quadrant I, highlight them in *gray* on your calendar. For activities that fall in quadrant III, highlight them in *yellow* on your calendar. For activities that fall in quadrant IV, highlight them in *red* on your calendar. Finally, for activities that fall in quadrant II, highlight them in *green* on your calendar. If you don't want to highlight

---

[77]   Ibid.

your activities in colors, simply put the appropriate descriptor (QI, QII, QIII, or QIV) next to the activity.

At the end of the week, analyze how you spent your time. You may be surprised with the results. Remember, quadrant II activities are intentional choices we make but are often neglected because of the tyranny of the urgent. We desire to be proactive with our lives but instead spend most of our time reacting to life or the demands of our responsibilities and obligations. By devoting time in quadrant II, you will find that you are moving from a desperate attempt to maintain balance to one of centered living.

QUESTIONS TO PONDER

What percentage of your time is spent in each quadrant?

What activities are you engaged in that waste time or are not healthy?

What changes must take place if you are to manage your time more effectively?

What kinds of activities will you prioritize for quadrant II?

RECOMMENDED RESOURCE

First Things First (1996) by Stephen R. Covey

POWER (THE IMPORTANCE OF INFLUENCE)

Each of us possesses power to influence outcomes within our sphere of influence for good or bad.

Our power base may arise from positional, personal, or spiritual authority. Power is not the production of intended effects, the ability to apply force, the intended and successful control of others, or the extent to which A can get B to do something that B normally would not do. Power is our influence potential.

Power is the resource that enables individuals to induce compliance from others or to influence them because of the positions the individuals hold, the people they know, the character and charisma they possess, the expertise they have, the experience they have built, the competencies they hold, the reputation they enjoy, and the knowledge they have acquired.

POWER BASES

A person exercises power and influence in essentially three broad areas of authority and influence: positional, personal, or spiritual.

Positional authority and influence is given from the top down, connected with the position we hold and the authority delegated to us based on our job descriptions and enforced from the assigning organization. In the corporate world, such power holds sway because opposing this surrogate power has consequences: reprimand, probation, demotion, or loss of a job.

Personal authority and influence is earned and given from the bottom up because of the individual characteristics we possess associated with our personalities, track records, knowledge, competence, proficiency, effectiveness, motivation, or inspiration we wield. People refer to us because of our stature and status.

Spiritual authority, the highest form of power and influence, is not earned but temporarily assigned by God, based on a vibrant relationship with him. It carries with it a sense of being God-anointed. It can be felt when we enter a room. Our force of modeling and moral expertise is recognized. Have you ever been in the presence of someone who emanates spiritual authority? Such people wear it like a mantle; you sense it and feel its influence. Two people quickly come to mind—the Reverend Billy Graham and Mother Teresa.

Spiritual power and authority comes to a person in three ways: (1) through an experiential knowledge of God and deep experiences with God, (2) through a life that demonstrates godliness, characterized by evidence of spiritual fruit, and (3) through gifted power, a clear testimony to divine intervention in one's ministry.

The resources brought to bear in the exercise of authority might include individual and collective assets, such as organization, money, reputation, personal appeal, persuasion skills, interpersonal skills, kinds of knowledge, information, the indwelling Holy Spirit, and giftedness. The degree of authority the leader possesses is directly proportional to the credibility the leader has with those he or she wishes to lead.

POWER STYLES

The dark side of power and influence is experienced when force or manipulation is used to gain compliance. The light side of power and influence is experienced when persuasion and legitimate authority is used to gain acceptance and agreement.

The style or form used to exercise influence often depends on our temperament, leadership style, learned practices, modeling of other leaders we respect, and spiritual maturity. More specifically, a leader's central belief system, core values, worldview (perceptual attitudes), and primary motives will often influence which style or form the leader uses.

For example, if a leader has a driver-type temperament, he or she may gravitate to force or manipulation. If a leader has an expressive or amiable temperament, he or she may use persuasion to influence others. A leader may admire another leader and therefore adapt or adopt that leader's style accordingly.

A leader's central belief system (Christian, secular) establishes his or her core values. Core values—the principles we live by—informs the set of perceptual attitudes or worldview we use to interpret and understand our observations of life around us. Our worldview conditions the primary motives behind behaviors observed by others. So the substance of these internal factors determines the use of one style over another.

Finally, the status and vibrancy of our relationship with Christ, our active pursuit of meaningful fellowship with the Father, and our reliance upon empowerment from the Holy Spirit will determine, in great measure, the degree of spiritual authority we hold and the spiritual influence we have over a specific group of God's people, in accordance with his purposes.

POWER TYPES[78]

Let's look at seven types of power. The first four are generally associated with those holding positional power and authority, while the last three deals with those holding personal power and authority. These types were described by J. Robert Clinton in *Leadership Emergence Theory.*

Coercive power is the perceived ability to employ sanctions, punishment, or consequences for not complying. Threats of force or of punishment often attend the exercise of this type of power.

Coercive power is not always a bad thing. For instance, when

---

[78]   J. Robert Clinton, *Leadership Emergence Theory: A Self-Study Manual for Analyzing the Development of a Christian Leader* (Altadena: Barnabas Publishers, 1989), 192–193.

there is danger involved or someone's safety is at stake, orders must be followed. The military in war operates from this type of power base. In the church, a pastor or ministry director may use this power base when a child's welfare is threatened, or legal sanctions must be adhered to for their protection.

Coercive power is eroded when used continually but without delivering the punishment promised or threatened. In other words, a person is warned but no action is taken. The threat of consequences diminishes because there is no follow-through with penalty for violating policy or procedures.

Connection power is the perception that a person knows and is associated with people of influence or has access to organizational resources who can be mobilized to exert power in a given situation or provide pressure to comply.

Connection power is eroded when people begin to see that the sponsor or connection does not make any disciplinary interventions or provide any favors or sanctions. If the word gets out that the leader doesn't garner respect from those above, then his or her authority quickly wanes, and his or her influence is reduced as a result.

Inducement (reward) power is the perceived ability to provide resources or perks, promises or rewards, or some favor sought by followers. This only works when a person can deliver what he or she has promised.

This type of power is eroded when everyone gets the same reward, whether they perform or not, or because they have seniority, or because it's someone else's turn. It also erodes when the leader can't deliver on his or her promises.

Legitimate power is when a person in authority exercises that authority in association with his or her job description, position in the organization, or role and the power he or she has been given through legitimate channels to carry out responsibilities, obligations, and duties. This type of power often fails when a person is given responsibility without the authority to carry it out.

Legitimate power is eroded by not making decisions that people think should be made, given their position. If the leader fails to exercise the authority given to him or her, then respect and compliance are adversely affected.

Competency power is the perception that the leader possesses expertise, a set of skills, or competencies or information necessary to the success of the organization. The information the person has or the competencies he/she enjoys is useful and necessary to the organization to get the job done or to successfully complete a project. The person's education, special certification, or relevant experience is helpful to the team or the enterprise as a whole.

Competency power is eroded when the leader gives away information or expertise to people whose goals are not organizational goals, uses information or his/her expertise as a means of impressing those being led to garner their admiration and respect, or to serve his/her own selfish agenda. Withholding information or expertise for a personal reason also can erode influence or produce resentment in others.

Personal (referent) power is the perceived appeal of being associated with an individual based on a recognition of that person's charisma, skills, and abilities. Those desiring such an association want to be seen with this person or to say they know him or her to gain some notoriety or access to other people and resources unavailable otherwise.

This type of power base is eroded when strokes or access are given to those who are not performing or such power breeds sycophants. This type of power can also produce yes-people who are unwilling to disagree for fear of alienation.

In the context of a ministry team, the team leader will increase his or her strength of influence by addressing primarily five dynamic factors.

1. Personal credibility (confidence, energy, dependability, decisiveness, positive attitude, sensitivity, willingness to assume responsibility, follow-through)
2. Legitimate authority (willingness to exercise authority, judicious and appropriate use of authority, faithfulness, good communication, engagement appropriate for a given situation)

3. Relational investment (appreciation, affirmation, acknowledgement, listening, support, buffering, removing barriers, allegiance, loyalty, awareness, forgiveness, repentance, respect, resourcing)

4. Psychological rewards (affirmation, honor, goal achievement, advancement, friendship, support, sponsorship, mentorship, more responsibility, more authority, recognition, constructive criticism)

5. Spiritual power (authenticity, integrity, spiritual maturity, reverence, example, modeling, humility, godliness, prayerfulness, respect from others, conviction, beliefs, values, attitude, virtue)

This chapter focused on the importance of understanding and properly using power, authority, and influence to facilitate God's redemptive work in our lives and in the lives of others whom God has called us to serve for his glory and honor.

Generally, the power base a leader uses to exercise his or her influence draws its utility from underlying resources, such as temperament, giftedness, personal appeal, knowledge, interpersonal skills, and so on. The degree to which leaders possess such power and the influence they wield in the exercise of their power is called authority. Some leaders have more authority than others. The style by which they exercise power can range from the use of force to manipulation, persuasion, or use of authority means. The scope of their authority and influence may be extended in three areas: direct influence, organizational influence, and indirect influence. Several types of power may be used to influence others, from coercive power to spiritual power. Spiritual power and authority is the preferred type for ministry leaders. As leaders grow, their spheres of influence—direct, indirect, and organizational—also grow.

Leaders can increase the strength of their influence by addressing five dynamic factors: personal credibility, legitimate authority, relational investment, psychological rewards, and the exercise of spiritual power.

QUESTIONS TO PONDER

What power base do you most often exercise?

What power type is your default pattern?

What kind of power will you strive to cultivate?

What can you do to increase your influence within your sphere of influence?

RECOMMENDED RESOURCE

Spiritual Influence: The Hidden Power Behind Leadership (2012) by Mel Lawrenz

CENTERING (LIVING A CENTERED VERSUS A BALANCED LIFE)

Don't you hate surveys? I do too. But the wonderful thing about being the teacher is that you get to ask people to do what you hate to do. Let's take a survey.

1. What percent of your time is spent of the following activities?

   - Your daily responsibilities
   - Others demands and crises
   - Recreation and escape
   - Personal planning and development

2. What percent of your time is spent with the following people?

   - Work associates
   - Friends
   - Self
   - Family

> Be careful, then, how you live—not as unwise but as wise, making the most of every opportunity, because the days are evil. (Ephesians 5:15–16)

Time is a precious resource. It cannot be saved or stored; it can only be used. Time that is not used is lost forever; it can never be recovered. Everyone has twenty-four hours per day.

Should we strive for balance? Is a balanced life possible? Does life happen to us in a predictable manner? Is all of life under our control? Life comes at us in unpredictable ways. Sometimes we see it coming. Other times it takes us by surprise. Sometimes we're prepared. Other times we are not prepared. What has happened in your life that caught you by surprise and threw you for a loop—something you didn't know was coming, something that knocked you off balance?

Picture yourself on a tightrope. What would your mind be on? What would be the state of your body? What would happen if a gust of wind hit you from the left? From the right? Would you be able to relax? What would be your primary focus? Our desire is to get from point A to point B without falling. While doing so, we are under anxiety and stress; our bodies are tense and on constant alert. We make myriad adjustments to maintain our balance. We rearrange the aspects of our lives in a new order. We reprioritize our activities. We constantly adjust our undertakings for the new reality. Maintaining balance amid life's circumstances is difficult, if not impossible, to achieve. Life happens to us in very unpredictable ways that can knock us off balance.

If living a balanced life is futile, how are we then to live? I recommend you consider living a *centered* life instead.

> For there is a proper time and procedure for every matter, though a man's misery weighs heavily upon him. (Ecclesiastes 8:6)

Christ was never in a hurry. When we look at the earthly life of Jesus, we don't see a harried, haphazard, and reactive lifestyle. No, we see a proactive, centered life. Crowds pressed in on him, and people clamored for his attention. His disciples urged his involvement. The Bible says that Jesus often withdrew to lonely places and prayed.[79] He was never harried, even when his friend Lazarus died.[80] He commended Mary to her sister Martha for choosing the right thing to do while she was distracted by many things.[81] Christ was centered because He knew his priority—to do the will of his Father and to finish his work.[82] He knew his priorities and ordered his life to fulfill those priorities.

We have a choice to live reactively or proactively, to live in accordance with God's plans or our plans, to live in alignment with his purposes for us or other's purposes for us, and to live by the clock or by the compass.

How does a spinning top maintain its equilibrium against opposing forces? When it is hit, it momentarily is knocked off equilibrium but soon regains its upright posture. It automatically finds its center of gravity.

What does a centered life look like? What is your spiritual center of gravity? Is it so strong that you're able to find your equilibrium, no matter what life throws at you? What do we know about this spiritual center of gravity? It has the following four essential elements that build one on the other:

1. A personal relationship with Christ
2. Biblical beliefs and values
3. A Christian worldview
4. Pure motives

It influences all life's activities and interactions—physical, emotional, intellectual, relational, professional, and spiritual. Once we know our personal spiritual center of gravity, we should order our lives accordingly.

Living a centered life is an inside-out process. Who we are at the

---

[79] Luke 5:16.

[80] Luke 11:6.

[81] Luke 10:40–42.

[82] John 4:34.

core of our beings will determine the quality of our behavior in the workplace, in the realm of our relationships, and in the sanctity of our homes. Our beingness dramatically influences our doingness. What we do does not determine who we are! Who we are determines the significance and effectiveness of what we do.

Living a centered life is living life by a compass, not by the clock. The clock represents our commitments, appointments, schedules, goals, and activities—these drive our behavior and condition our responses. The compass represents our vision, values, principles, mission, direction and destiny—what we feel is important; what we believe should lead our lives.

QUESTIONS TO PONDER

Are you living your life proactively or reactively?

What is the condition of your inner core?

How do your beliefs and values impact your behavior?

Do you live your life by the clock or the compass?

What changes do you need to make to live a centered life?

RECOMMENDED RESOURCE

The Jesus-Centered Life: The Life You Didn't Think Possible, With the Jesus You Never Knew (2016) by Rick Lawrence

FOCUSING (FINDING YOUR UNIQUE TRAJECTORY)

The recent loss of a close friend and peer mentor and the struggle of another close friend with three heart attacks in quick succession have reminded me again how valuable yet fleeting life is and how important it is not to waste what God has intended for our lives; how important it is to focus on what matters.

In scripture we find this warning: "So, then, be careful how you live. Do not be unwise but wise, making the best use of your time because the times are evil. Therefore, do not be foolish, but understand what the Lord's will is."[83]

Regarding this issue, I've learned a few lessons on my journey of almost seven decades.

Life is fleeting; don't waste it. How much time is spent on things that don't really matter? As I look over my life, I am alarmed at how quickly it has passed. "Now listen, you who say, Today or tomorrow we will go to such and such a town, stay there a year, conduct business, and make money. You do not know what tomorrow will bring. What is your life? You are a mist that appears for a little while and then vanishes."[84]

---

[83] Ephesians 5:15–17.

[84] James 4:13–14.

Our existence and the days that have been apportioned are predetermined by God. We are not mistakes, coincidences, or fate. We were on the heart of God before we ever came to be. "For You formed my inward parts; You wove me in my mother's womb. I will give thanks to You, for I am fearfully and wonderfully made; wonderful are Your works, and my soul knows it very well. My frame was not hidden from You, when I was made in secret, and skillfully wrought in the depths of the earth; Your eyes have seen my unformed substance; and in Your book, were all written the days that were ordained for me, when as yet there was not one of them."[85] "Teach us to number our days, that we may gain a heart of wisdom."[86]

God has a unique and personal purpose for our lives. Amazingly, he determined it before we ever came to be. He prepared our lives in advance. "For we are God's handiwork, created in Christ Jesus to do good works, which God prepared in advance for us to do."[87] We have a calling we need to engage. "I therefore, a prisoner for the Lord, urge you to walk in a manner worthy of the calling to which you have been called, with all humility and gentleness, with patience, bearing with one another in love, eager to maintain the unity of the Spirit in the bond of peace."[88] Our calling and the gifts he has given us to implement that calling are unalterable. "For the gifts and the calling of God are irrevocable."[89]

Every follower of Christ has a ministry to accomplish. Ministry is not just for the professionals. Scripture tells us that each of us is a minister of reconciliation.[90] We all have a ministry to fulfill. Rick Warren, senior pastor of Saddleback Church in Lake Forest, California, preached a sermon about the fact that everyone is a minister.

We've been created for ministry, saved for ministry, called to

---

85   Psalm 139:1–18.
86   Psalm 90:12.
87   Ephesians 2:10.
88   Ephesians 4:1–3.
89   Romans 11:29.
90   2 Corinthians 5:16–20.

ministry, gifted for ministry, and commanded to minister. The body of Christ needs our ministry, and we are called to be ministers of reconciliation.[91] It comes with this admonition: "See to it that you complete the work you have received from the Lord."[92]

We have been gifted by God for the ministry he has given us. Our giftedness includes spiritual gifts, natural abilities (talents), acquired skills, personality temperament, leadership style, core values, and operational principles. Coming to clarity regarding these issues will bring focus and intentionality to our lives.

So how do we find the path we are to tread? How do we determine the trajectory our lives should take? How do we bring focus to our lives? How do we engage in what eternally matters?

I would suggest you develop a personal life mandate that includes your biblical purpose, life purpose, committed passion, role nonnegotiables, unique methodologies, and ultimate contribution. Together they will provide a clear path ahead, the journey you were destined to take and that God equipped you to take. I have taken many people through the process of developing a personal life mandate. Each one of them was excited to take the journey, once they knew what God had planned for them.

FOCUSED LIFE

Beginning with an all-out commitment to God, a focused life is a life dedicated to exclusively carrying out God's unique purposes through it by identifying the focal issues; that is, biblical purpose, life purpose, committed passion, nonnegotiables, unique methodology, and ultimate contribution that allows and increases prioritization of life's activities around the focal issues and results in a satisfying life of being and doing.

---

[91] Ephesians 2:10; 2 Timothy 1:8–11; Ephesians 4:1; 1 Peter 2:5–10; 1 Peter 4:10; 1 Corinthians 12:4–7; Matthew 20:26–28; Colossians 4:17; Ephesians 6:7–8; Hebrews 9:14; 1 Corinthians 12:27; Matthew 9:36–38; 2 Corinthians 5:16–20.

[92] Colossians 4:17.

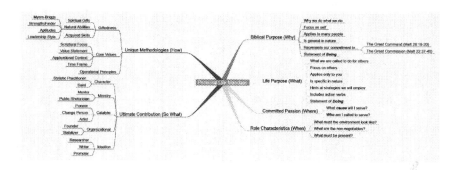

BIBLICAL PURPOSE (FUEL)

A biblical purpose addresses one's beingness—the energy that compels one's doingness. It informs, conditions, and influences one's life purpose. It is the fuel for the engine of one's God-ordained activities and engagement. Those who seek to live a focused life of significance and meaning must determine the foundation of that life—what will affect the carrying out of one's life purpose. A biblical purpose establishes the resources that will provide the impetus for biblically informed action going forward.

LIFE PURPOSE (FOCUS)

One's life purpose is a burden-like calling, a task or driving force or achievement, which motivates a leader to fulfill something or to see something done. Frequently, leaders will have one to three dominant life purposes, some combination of one or more, or at least an umbrella one that is clarified by more detailed sub purposes. Life purpose is the dominant focal issue in a leader's life. The following principles apply:

1. A leader cannot have a focused life apart from a life purpose that lies at the core of his/her being. Life purpose, however, is not enough to generate a focused life.
2. Life purpose forms the prime integrating factor around which a focused life operates. The seeds of life purpose are contained in a leader's unusual experiences with God. These experiences are called sense-of-destiny experiences. All leaders have a sense of destiny.

3. Various means are used by God to intervene in leaders' lives to create a sense of destiny and bring clarity to their life purposes. Destiny processing provides the seedbed for discovering life purpose. A study of destiny processing will provide insights into life purpose. The four types of destiny processing are as follows:

- Awe-inspiring experiences (e.g., Isaiah's experience in Isaiah 6)
- Indirect-destiny experiences (e.g., dedication of Samuel in 1 Samuel 1)
- Providential circumstances (e.g., Barnabas and Paul, Acts 4)
- The blessing of God over time (e.g., Joseph's life, Genesis 39)

COMMITTED PASSION (CALLING)

Committed passion is a focused, intentional, energized action defined by your inner drive to fulfill your revealed destiny and to be all God has equipped and wired you to be. Life purpose without the follow-through of committed passion is merely a dream with little chance of becoming a reality. It's the magnetism that causes your internal compass needle to point to true north. It's the dedication and devotion to realizing your full created potential. Committed passion is a people group that God has called you to serve, a cause he has called you to embrace, or a combination of both.

ROLE NONNEGOTIABLES (BOUNDARIES)

Role nonnegotiables refers to the official or unofficial position, status, platform, leadership function, or job description that basically describes what a leader does and that allows recognition by others; it uniquely fits who a leader is and allows that leader effectively accomplish a life purpose. It's a place where 80 percent of who you are overlaps 80 percent of what you do.

Regardless of role, what are the nonnegotiables that must be present for you to thrive and not be thwarted from what God has called you to be and do?

A major role recognizes that we may not be able to carry out our life purpose and exploit our unique methodologies unless we have the freedom to adjust our present role. A major role usually will have to be adapted. Organizations rarely define such a role to fit a person. The major role may be a combination of formally recognized functions related to a position or qualifications, as well as informal ones done implicitly within the functions of a job description or in addition to the job description.

A suitable major role is one that enhances giftedness and allows use of unique methodologies that will lead to ultimate contributions—a legacy. The giftedness set includes natural abilities, acquired skills, and spiritual gifts. Natural abilities refer to those capacities, skills, talents, or aptitudes that are innate in a person and allow him/her to accomplish things.

Acquired skills refer to those capacities, skills, talents, or aptitudes that have been learned by a person to allow him/her to accomplish something. A spiritual gift is a God-given unique capacity imparted to each believer for releasing a Holy Spirit-empowered ministry via that believer and that produces supernatural results.

In early stages, it is necessary to try out many varying assignments to really discover your giftedness and which roles your giftedness best match. As you experience several miniconvergences over time, and as you get a better understanding of your giftedness, you will know the ideal role for you. A major role represents the best fit between your giftedness and the job you must do. This major role allows for effective use of unique methodologies and the satisfaction of a fulfilling life purpose.

UNIQUE METHODOLOGIES (TOOL KIT)

A unique methodology is ministry insight around which the leader can pass on to others the essentials of doing something, using something, or being something; that is, a means of effectively delivering the important ministry of that leader, which enhances life purpose(s) or moves toward ultimate contribution. It represents repeated use of a ministry insight and recognition that the ministry insight should be used with effectiveness.

Unique methodologies are those ministry insights that fit who we are, help us carry out our life purposes, and become effective vehicles for us to carry out ministry. They are the tools we have been given to implement our life purposes and committed passion. They may include an approach, a method, a design, a technique, a philosophy, a framework, a format, a concept, a procedure, a process, a strategy, an ability, or developed materials.

Unique methodologies describe the major means whereby life purpose and/or ultimate contributions are realized. These relate to how we operate or the means whereby we achieve or make progress in delivering our ministry.

Unique methodologies include but are not limited to spiritual gifts, natural abilities (talents), acquired skills, personality temperament, leadership style, core values, and engagement principles we have learned along the way. When employed, God moves in dynamic ways.

ULTIMATE CONTRIBUTION (LEGACY)

An ultimate contribution is a lasting legacy of a Christian, for which he or she is remembered and which furthers the cause of Christianity by one or more of the following means:

- Setting standards for life and ministry
- Impacting lives by enfolding them in God's kingdom or developing them once in God's kingdom
- Serving as a stimulus for change that betters the world
- Leaving behind an organization, institution, or movement that will further channel God's work
- The discovery of ideas, communication of them, or promotion of them so that they further God's work

An ultimate contribution is a legacy that a leader leaves behind after life is over. It is possible to leave several ultimate contributions. An ultimate contribution helps set the boundaries for what we want to accomplish in terms of the big picture. They will relate to the means and ends. They might include a model godly life, a model ministry style, a mentor who helps people realize their potential, a communicator of truth, a teacher, a pioneer in some new area, a change person who rights wrongs and injustices, an innovator or creator of breakthroughs, an entrepreneur who starts an endeavor to meet a need, a stabilizer who solidifies an organization or ministry, a researcher who develops new ideation, a writer who captures ideas in written form, a promoter who distributes new ideas or ministry concepts, or anything that leaves a legacy from which others benefit.

We are encouraged to redeem the time, to make every moment count, to facilitate God's redemptive purposes in a fallen world.[93] An evaluation is coming at the judgment seat of Christ, at which time we will give an account for what we have done with what we have been given. We will be recompensed for what we have contributed that eternally matters.[94] This is not a judgment of your fitness for the kingdom or your eternal security. That has been assured by Christ. He remembers our sins no more.[95] The enemy wants to remind us of the failures of our past. God wants to bring us to the victories of our future. The battle is for the present, but God is God, and Satan is not.

QUESTIONS TO PONDER

What is your God-ordained wiring?
What is your life purpose?
What is your personal life mandate?
What do you intend to do about it?

RECOMMENDED RESOURCE

Setting Your Course: How to Navigate Your Life's Journey (2014) by Dr. Greg Bourgond

---

[93] Psalm 90:12, 17; Ephesians 5:15–16.
[94] 2 Corinthians 5:10; Romans 14:10; 1 Corinthians 3:11–15.
[95] Hebrews 8:12; 10:17; Isaiah 38:17; 43:25; Jeremiah 31:34; Romans 4:8.

AUDITING (ASSESSING YOUR SPIRITUAL VITALITY)

Conducting a personal spiritual audit will help you reflect, assess, evaluate, and realign the trajectory of your journey. Every now and then, it is helpful to appraise your life and compare it to your intended objectives.

The primary purpose of a personal spiritual audit is to determine the current status of your well-being from a biblical point of view. Depending on your personal alignment (or battle) plan, your personal life mandate, or any other development plan you may have produced and attempted to implement, a regularly scheduled time away for reflective assessment and evaluation is very important.

The goal of this time is to truthfully come to clarity regarding your progress, honestly admit failure where applicable, determine course corrections, and recommit to implementing a revised plan of engagement. Sharing this plan with a trusted friend or ally for purposes of counsel, advice, and accountability will help you live out your conclusions. After all, a demonstrated godly life in accordance with Titus 2:11–14 is your primary objective.

> For the grace of God that brings salvation has appeared
> to all men. It teaches us to say "No" to ungodliness and

worldly passions, and to live self-controlled, upright and godly lives in this present age, while we wait for the blessed hope—the glorious appearing of our great God and Savior, Jesus Christ, who gave himself for us to redeem us from all wickedness and to purify for himself a people that are his very own, eager to do what is good. (Titus 2:11–14)

One of the best ways to conduct a personal spiritual audit is a silent retreat of two to three days. This may seem a bit scary at first but will prove to be enormously helpful in the long run. The first day should be a day of rest, punctuated by several naps.

Why? Because most of us are living adrenaline-fueled lives of hectic and harried activity. Most of us live in the "tyranny of the urgent." We spend our days bouncing from one emergency to the next, one crisis to the next, one problem to the next. with little time to catch our breath.

The following natural cycle is recommended, whether you go on a silent retreat or carve away time for intentional reflection, assessment, evaluation, and realignment.

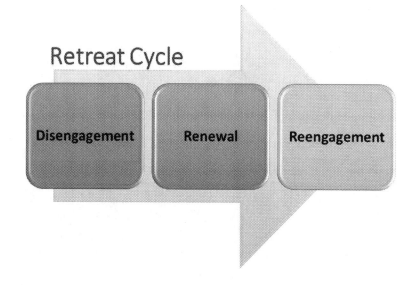

Retreat Cycle

| Disengagement | Renewal | Reengagement |

DISENGAGEMENT

Regardless of the format for your getaway, healthy disengagement is critical to the process. This may translate into any activity that represents downtime (such as naps, walks, hikes, or the like) that does not require any detailed preparation or planning. The key is to disengage and rest for several hours to a day before renewal can take place. You may experience achy muscles or some other physical phenomenon that indicates your body is going through adrenaline withdrawal. Stay away from any stressful activity during this phase, including stressful thoughts or conflictive situations. The goal is to rest and relax—period.

RENEWAL

At the beginning of this phase you may want to complete one or more personal evaluations, surveys, or questionnaires to assess where you are currently. The following instruments will help you with this initial assessment:

- Five-habits checklist[96]
- Conduct a spiritual audit—twelve questions to ask yourself[97]
- Spiritual audit[98]

A SPIRITUAL LIFE CHECKUP

Set aside an hour of uninterrupted time to thoughtfully answer the following statements. Circle the number to the left that indicates to what extent that statement is true in your life: never (1), maybe (2), sometimes (3), often (4), always (5). The results will help you to have a

---

[96]   Greg Bourgond, *Setting Your Course: How to Navigate Your Life's Journey* (Bloomington: iUniverse LLC, 2014), 351–353.

[97]   Fred Smith, "Conducting a Spiritual Audit: 12 Questions to Keep Your Personal Accounts in Order," *Leadership*, Winter 1998, www.thelifethatlistens.com/other/Conducting_a_Spiritual_Audit.doc.

[98]   Brian Harris, "Conducting a Spiritual Audit: A First Fifteen of Questions…," *Brian Harris*, October 20, 2015, http://brianharrisauthor.com/conducting-a-spiritual-audit-a-first-fifteen-of-questions/.

better understanding of your spiritual life and to plan for your spiritual care. You may want to share your answers with your mentor or spiritual director.

o   My personal relationship with God is intimate.

o   I practice various spiritual disciplines (prayer, meditation, Bible reading, fasting, etc.) in my spiritual life.

o   I take time off for retreats to refresh myself spiritually and physically.

o   I believe my devotional time influences my lifestyle.

o   I have a daily time of devotions with my family.

o   I feel I apply biblical principles to my daily living.

o   I give tithes and offerings to my church.

o   I believe fellowship with fellow Christians is necessary.

o   I can "sense" the presence of the Lord in corporate worship.

o   I spend time interceding for others.

o   I pray for missions, the unreached people, etc.

o   I have someone with whom to share my joys, dreams, needs, and burdens.

o   I have a regular time for family, recreation, personal growth, etc.

o   I have a healthy self-image.

o   I know how to deal with pressure and crisis in life.

o   I feel I can stand strong against temptations (impatience, anger, greed, lust, etc.).

o   I am a forgiving, loving, and accepting person.

o   I am sure of my calling, and I enjoy my ministry.

o   I exercise my spiritual gifts regularly.

o   I share my faith with others.

o   I have a burden for the needy and will offer a helping hand.

o   I regularly attend a course to broaden my perspective and knowledge on Christian spirituality.

o   The Holy Spirit plays a vital role in my life and ministry.

THE BARREL EXERCISE[99]

> I am the gate; whoever enters through me will be saved. He will come in and go out, and find pasture. The thief comes only to steal and kill and destroy; I have come that they may have life, and have it to the full. (John 10:9–10)

> "For I know the plans I have for you," declares the LORD, "plans to prosper you and not to harm you, plans to give you hope and a future." (Jeremiah 29:11–12)

> Finally, brothers, whatever is true, whatever is noble, whatever is right, whatever is pure, whatever is lovely, whatever is admirable—if anything is excellent or praiseworthy—think about such things. (Philippians 4:8–9)

> Do not conform any longer to the pattern of this world but be transformed by the renewing of your mind. Then you will be able to test and approve what God's will is—his good, pleasing and perfect will. (Romans 12:2)

Every person has a reservoir of physical, emotional, and spiritual energy. We'll call it your "barrel." If the rate of drainage exceeds the rate of filling, your energy dissipates and can lead to anxiety, fear, paranoia, and neurotic behavior.

Certain things can drain your barrel, such as day-to-day responsibilities, obligations, and duties. Some of these things are natural and expected, such as your job, family, and life in general. Bad decisions, dysfunctional activity, unhealthy habits, and sin can drain your barrel. Personal conflicts, workaholism, and addictions also can drain your barrel.

What legitimately drains your barrel? What dysfunctional behaviors

---

[99] Adapted from Wayne Cordeiro, Self-Leadership, Willow Creek Summit (2011).

drain your barrel? What self-induced actions drain your barrel? What draining actions can you eliminate?

Certain activities can fill your barrel, such as devotions, prayer, spiritual renewal, true recreation. Other activities that fill your barrel might include bike riding, skating, cooking, hiking, reading, or fishing, for instance. Healthy habits can provide the energy you need to function effectively and live an abundant life. What physical activities fill your barrel? What emotional activities fill your barrel? What intellectual activities fill your barrel? What spiritual activities fill your barrel? What life-giving activities can you add that will fill your barrel?

Be sure to bring your Bible to read and a journal to record your insights and findings. Capture your thoughts on paper. Journaling will help you seize the divine moments that will come when you are still enough to hear the "still small voice" of God. Why does God speak so profoundly in a still small voice? Because it forces us to lean forward to hear it. *Leaning forward* means to proactively remove any distractions and interference so we can tune our hearts to the heart of God. And that means to put away all—and I mean all—electronics, such as you cell phone, computer, iPad, and iPod.

Record in your journal what you hear from God, such as insights gleaned; knowledge gained; clarifications made; questions to ponder; lessons learned; God's prompting; examples to follow; sins to avoid; promises to claim; relationships to restore; forgiveness to offer; prayers to repeat; commands to obey; conditions to meet; plans to implement; verses to memorize; errors to observe; challenges to face; knowledge to acquire about God, Christ, or yourself; stumbling blocks to remove; or actions to take.

REENGAGEMENT

At the end of your silent retreat or getaway, consolidate your takeaways and key findings. Draft your implementation plan—what you intend to do with what you heard from the Lord. Remember, we overestimate what we can accomplish in the short term, and we underestimate what we can accomplish in the long term.

Conducting a spiritual audit will help you recenter your life, find your equilibrium, and determine what will inform and condition your life and what will guide your journey ahead, regardless of your pursuits.

QUESTIONS TO PONDER

What was the one big thing I learned?
Where did I hear God's still small voice?
What new understandings did I attain?
What do I intend to do about what I have learned?
Who will hold me accountable for the journey ahead?

RECOMMENDED RESOURCE

Renovation of the Heart: Putting on the Character of Christ (2012) by Dallas Willard

HAND

LEADING (HOW TO COME TO TERMS WITH BEING A LEADER)

We are all leaders by default. You may not see yourself as a leader. You may be a reluctant leader. You may be a person who has learned to be a leader. Or you may be a natural leader. There are times when you are a follower and other times a leader. But make no mistake about it—everyone leads at some time, whether on the job or in the home, completing a project or volunteering your time. Any time you make or implement a decision that impacts others, you are leading. On any given day, you can find examples of good leadership or bad leadership.

One scholar has noted that *leadership* is the most observed and least understood phenomenon on earth. Attempts to define a leader or leadership represent multiple perspectives.

- There are only three kinds of people in the world—those who are immovable, those who are moveable, and those who move them.
- Leadership is a relationship in which one person seeks to influence the behaviors, beliefs, attitudes, or values of another. In the context of organizational management, leadership is a relationship of influence with the twin objectives of accomplishing a task and developing the people.

- Leadership is the ability and the activity of influencing people and of shaping their behavior.
- A leader is someone you will follow to a place you wouldn't go by yourself.
- A leader is a person who influences people to accomplish a purpose.

During my doctoral work, I reviewed over three hundred definitions of a leader and leadership. One common theme repeated itself in many of the definitions I reviewed—influence. In the New Testament, we are called to influence others for kingdom purposes. That being the case, we are all leaders by default.

The questions, then, are as follows:

- How well do you lead when given an opportunity to do so?
- What and/or who informs how you lead?
- What stands in a privileged position of authority over your leadership?
- What conditions and shapes the exercise of your leadership?"

From my point of view, Dr. J. Robert Clinton (1989), professor emeritus of leadership for the School of World Mission of Fuller Theological Seminary, does the best job defining leadership and a leader from a biblical point of view. He defines *leadership* as follows:

> Leadership is a dynamic process over an extended period in various situations in which a leader utilizing leadership resources and by specific leadership behaviors, influences the thoughts and activities of followers toward accomplishment of aims usually mutually beneficial for leaders, followers, and the macro context of which they are a part.[100]

---

[100] J. Robert Clinton, *Leadership Emergence Theory: A Self-Study Manual for Analyzing the Development of a Christian Leader* (Altadena: Barnabas Publishers,

It's his definition of a leader, however, that captures the significance of being God's leader for me.

> A leader is a person with a God-given capacity and a God-given responsibility to influence a specific group of God's people toward his purposes for the group.[101]

Regardless of which definition you prefer, one word is repeated frequently and is at the heart of leadership—*influence*! Let's examine J. Robert Clinton's definition as a leader more closely.

A leader, as defined from a study of biblical leadership, is *a person with God-given capacity* (denotes giftedness capacity in terms of spiritual gifts, natural talents, and acquired skills and suggests leadership character as well as potential to be developed) *and with God-given responsibility* (denotes a downward sense of responsibility, a burden from God, to influence others for God, and an upward sense of responsibility, accountability to God, for the people being influenced), *who is influencing a specific group of God's people* (those to whom the leader is given charge by God, those he/she is responsible for and may include direct and indirect influence over them) *toward God's purposes for the group.* (The prime function of leadership is the influencing of groups to accomplish God's purposes involving the group. This requires vision.)

This external direction is what distinguishes a Christian leader from a secular leader. Christian leaders must move followers toward recognition of, acceptance of, and participation in bringing about that God-given vision.

A focus on leadership or a leader does not, in any way, diminish the role and function of a manager. Comparing a leader and a manager has often been reduced to a simplified contrast—leaders lead people, while managers manage things. Managers also manage people. The following

---

1989), 40.

[101] Ibid., 36.

comparison between leadership and management is more nuanced and accurate.

Leadership	Management
Sets vision	Implements vision
Provides motivation	Administrates
Sets standards	Implements standards
Conceptualizes	Organizes and plans
Personal authority required	Positional authority required
Future focused	Present focused
Grows and enhances	Arranges and tells

What is even more profound is the fact that God chooses his followers to facilitate his redemptive purposes in the world. He selects men and women to provide leadership and management to accomplish his agenda.

The quality of leadership and management expressed is totally dependent on what authority informs, conditions, and establishes it— the world, the flesh, the devil and his minions, or God. Sometimes great change benefitting others arises from despicable motives. The results do not, however, justify the means used to produce them. For instance, a company builds a factory in a depressed area, providing desperately needed jobs. The motive of the company, however, is to make as much money as possible, regardless of the harm it is doing to the environment through careless disposal of manufacturing waste that is polluting the water supply.

Motives matter. God judges the motives of our hearts. Scripture underscores the importance of motives.

- All a man's ways seem innocent to him, but motives are weighed by the Lord.[102]
- And you, my son Solomon, acknowledge the God of your father, and serve him with wholehearted devotion and with a willing mind, for the Lord searches every heart and understands every motive behind the thoughts.[103]
- Therefore, judge nothing before the appointed time; wait till the Lord comes. He will bring to light what is hidden in darkness and will expose the motives of men's hearts. At that time, each will receive his praise from God.[104]
- When you ask, you do not receive, because you ask with wrong motives, that you may spend what you get on your pleasures.[105]

You can be a leader and a follower simultaneously. You can lead formally and informally. You can lead without knowing you are leading. Let us reject the notion we are not leaders. You can be gifted to lead. You can learn how to lead. Any time you seek to change someone's mind, compel him/her to choose a different option, suggest a different approach, interject a better way, urge another to do something, set an example for others to follow, present an ideology or philosophy, encourage others to reach their potential, correct destructive behavior, or make a stand, you are leading, even if others disagree with you or do not listen to you.

Whether exercising positional, personal, or spiritual authority, you are leading. Positional authority is given to you from above by others and comes with the position or role you assume. Personal authority is given to you from below, based on your expertise, charisma, character, connections, or respect. Spiritual authority is given to you by God, based on your relationship to him and your spiritual maturity. It is not something you earn. God leases it to you for a season and can remove it

---

102 Proverbs 16:2.
103 1 Chronicles 28:9.
104 1 Corinthians 4:5.
105 James 4:3.

at any time, based on willful sin, spiritual abuse, or arrogance. Others will see it in you.

QUESTIONS TO PONDER

What informs the exercise of your leadership or management?
What authority do you rely on for guidance?
What motivates your leadership or management?
Who do you respect as a leader or manager?
What informs and motivates the leader or manager you respect?

RECOMMENDED RESOURCE

The Making of a Leader: Recognizing the Lessons and Stages of Leadership Development (2012) by Robert Clinton

REALIZING (HOW TO DRAW OUT UNREALIZED POTENTIAL)

One of the primary functions of leaders is to develop those under their charge. Keen powers of observation are necessary to uncover the potential within another person. Knowing someone's potential and helping him or her to realize it is one of the most rewarding experiences a leader can have.

When observing someone who reports to you or is within your sphere of relationships or influence, a leader should pay attention to strengths, limitations, and weaknesses. Intentional assessment of these areas will reveal a person's potential. The goal at this point is to encourage that person to explore his/her potential to discover that he/she has a greater capacity and capability than he/she may realize.

Individuals' strengths are composed of an amalgamation of their spiritual gifts, natural abilities, acquired skills, personality temperament, core values, discovered axiomatic operating principles, experience, and worldview. The configuration of these elements, the dominance of these factors, and the ways in which they are applied to events, circumstances, and situations make each individual just that—individually unique.

Although there exist a wide variety of instruments designed to reveal the many dimensions that make us human, observation of a person in a variety of settings will yield a relatively accurate picture of his/her

God-ordained design, what he/she offers, and how he/she can make the greatest contribution to a team, a vision, an objective, or a goal.

Limitations are not weaknesses. Limitations include one area that cannot be mediated and two that can. Individuals may not have the aptitude demanded of the responsibility they have been given. For instance, if they are put in charge of finances for a project and are required to manage a complex budget, yet they have no aptitude for numbers or financial structures, they may be doomed to failure. The two other areas include experience and training, both of which can be addressed by providing opportunities to gain experience or acquire the training necessary for success. So aptitude, experience, and training and the lack thereof is not a weakness; it is a limitation.

A weakness may be a character flaw, a compromised work ethic, a poor attitude, or the like. These weaknesses may also be mediated but will more than likely take time and patience before a person can conquer these inadequacies. As a leader, manager, or supervisor, you may not have the time to do so, especially when a short project deadline looms over the team.

Two factors repeatedly prevent someone from realizing his/her full potential—competence and confidence. Because of legitimate limitations or weaknesses, such as a lack of discipline, a person may experience varying degrees of performance that may adversely impact their competence and confidence, thereby affecting the subsequent successful completion of assigned tasks.

So developing your powers of observation can facilitate your ability to accurately assess someone's strengths, limitations, and weaknesses. An understanding of the unrealized potential resident in an individual will become apparent. Strategies can then be formulated to help individuals engage their unrealized potential so that they can enjoy new opportunities to exercise their newfound awareness. They may be hesitant at first to explore their potential, for fear of failure or simply because of unfamiliarity. The leader may have to exert influence, as a sage on the stage or a guide by the side, until the person is more comfortable in the exercise of his/her potential.

Leaders may have to adjust their leadership styles to accommodate the ability (competence) and readiness (confidence) of the person being led.

If team members are unable and unwilling or insecure, they may have to be directed and shown specifically how to accomplish the task, objective, or role. In this case, the leader simply describes the steps necessary to effectively and efficiently complete the task, objective, or role.

If the team members are unable but willing or confident, the leader might have to coach them through encouragement, empowerment, or exhortation. The leader may still make the final decision but will explain the rationale to the team members for learning purposes.

If the team member is able but unwilling or insecure, the leader may have to shift from a sage on the stage to a guide by the side, in which the team member is given the opportunity to make the decision with guidance and encouragement from the leader.

If the team member is able and willing or confident, the leader should delegate responsibility to the member, observe his/her performance, and offer timely advice and suggestions, as needed or requested.

You may recognize this adaptable leadership style as situational leadership.[106] One caution is needed at this point. Potential has a boundary. The worst thing a leader can do is to promote the notion that team members can do anything they set their minds to doing, if they are committed and disciplined. That, frankly, is not true. Team members can do whatever they have the capability and competence to do. Forcing individuals beyond their capabilities and competence will only break their spirits.

People should not be treated as tools or functionaries but as valuable resources imbued by their Creator to contribute in significant ways to worthwhile endeavors. Helping people realize their God-given potential can only help an organization to reach seemingly impossible dreams.

---

[106]   Ken Blanchard, Patricia Zigarmi, and Drea Zigarmi, *Leadership and the One Minute Manager Updated Ed: Increasing Effectiveness Through Situational Leadership II* (New York City: William Morrow, 2013).

QUESTIONS TO PONDER

What are the strengths of the people with whom you work?

What are the limitations and weaknesses of the people with whom you work?

What is the unrealized potential of the people with whom you work?

How are you helping people realize their unrealized potential?

RECOMMENDED RESOURCE

Developing the Leaders Around You: How to Help Others Reach Their Full Potential (2005) by John C. Maxwell

RECRUITING (HOW TO IDENTIFY EMERGING LEADERS)

I repeatedly hear the refrain "We don't have enough leaders." Emerging, budding leaders aren't obvious to others who do not have the eyes to see them. In fact, the characteristics of leaders in the rough are most often experienced as annoying aggravations rather than counterintuitive indicators. If the prevailing leaders within an organization do not calibrate their perceptions, they may never see the emerging leaders right in front of them.

If your identification "antenna" is not properly calibrated, you could miss the many leaders in your midst. Characteristics of emerging leaders often drive experienced leaders nuts, leading to premature dismissal of these nascent young leaders in the process of becoming, yet not having arrived. My experience suggests, however, that young leaders in the making possess observable behaviors that indicate they are potential leaders. They may need cultivation, training, mentoring, support, and sponsorship to develop into effective leaders. Your investment in them will be well worth the effort.

FIVE CHARACTERISTICS OF BUDDING LEADERS

1. Insistent: Budding leaders never give up.

They keep butting their heads against the same wall. You know the old saying "What is the definition of insanity? Doing the same thing over again and expecting different results." To someone observing emerging leaders, it sure looks like they are backtracking over the same problem again and again. Closer observation may show that they are hitting the wall at a slightly different angle each time, learning from each obstacle and adjusting their approach.

The key is that they don't give up, and they learn with each failure. There is a difference between this type of emerging leader and a lesser one. The lesser one always approaches the obstacle in exactly the same way and does not learn any lessons. They are more apt to give up after a few tries. Budding leaders are tenacious; they don't give up easily. View this characteristic in a positive light. Before jumping in, observe their behavior to determine their approaches to solving seemingly intractable problems. You might just have a great leader in the making.

2. Inquisitive: They are full of questions.

They never do exactly what you tell them to do. They keep asking more questions or even suggest ways it could be done better. They have more questions than you have answers. Man, that's irritating. Don't you just hate that? This is our typical response. Part of the role of leader, as leadership developer/mentor, is to suggest a direction and then work with the emerging leader on the approaches. Yes, it's irritating and time consuming, but it helps to grow a leader.

Often the mistake of mature leaders is in interpreting the attitudes and questions of a budding leader as disrespect and a critical spirit, rather than using these opportunities to learn about other ways to approach a problem themselves. You might find that their ideas are superior to your own. Budding leaders are inquisitive. Their questions may not be polished, leading you to conclude they are being insolent or that they are challenging you. Don't look at it that way. See their questions as exhibiting a desire to learn.

3. Impatient: They seek more responsibility before they may be ready.

As the mature leader, you are queasy about this. You want the person to advance as a leader, but you also have some doubts because you are not sure he/she is ready. If he/she exhibits the potential to lead and has been faithful in smaller projects in the past, then give the person an opportunity to stretch. If he/she fails, observe how he/she handles the failure. What has the person learned from it?

Their development might require a guide by the side, not a sage on the stage. Part of the development process is placing people in situations that are a true stretch. As leadership developers/mentors, we don't want to put people in places where they will fail. But if failure is not an option, they will not learn as fast as they can. Failure should be handled as a developmental iteration on the process to becoming a better leader. Seeking more responsibility, even if they are not ready for it, is a sure sign of a budding leader. Don't be impatient with their impatience.

4. Incognito: They are leaders by default.

People defer to them, even if they haven't been designated as the leader. They have been placed in a group or team to carry out a task. Someone else has been designated as leader, but as the project progresses, the group looks to this emerging leader for his/her opinion. This can be very hard on the designated leader, but the group doesn't seem to mind, unless there is a strong clash between the two.

These budding leaders aren't always obvious in group settings. They are often on the periphery, lurking just out of sight. They are exposed when others in the group look to them for approval or response. They may be reluctant leaders or not see themselves as leaders at all. They may be mavericks or contrarians. They may be quiet and reserved. They are, however, seen clearly by their peers as leaders.

Investigate how budding leaders are perceived by their peers and friends. Observe how they are engaged by others or deferred to by others. Observe how their influence is exercised. They may be rough or even difficult. Yet conscious development can make them effective leaders.

5. Innovative—They often go beyond what is asked of them.

Emerging leaders often do more than they are asked to do, sometimes to the point of overdoing it. Although this can be a sign to a senior leader that time and energy are being wasted, it is also a sign that the emerging leader is ready for more responsibility. The emerging leader is looking not to impress but rather to do the task or responsibility to his/her high standards. Sometimes those standards are higher than what we would have in mind if we were doing the project.

Observe how they adjust their leadership styles to fit the situation. Remember that their unique wiring may result in unique solutions. Give them room to operate. How do they adjust to a problem? What techniques do they employ in solving a problem? How do they engage others in resolving the situation? Innovation is taking what is and making it better. It is leveraging existing circumstances to produce a better outcome. A race horse must be trained to run within the rails and not damage itself in the process. Gentle guidance of innovators can ensure they excel within legitimate boundaries.

Careful observation of potential budding leaders can yield a bumper crop of future effective leaders if you have the patience and understanding of the characteristics they exhibit. You may have to provide a safe place for their development and act as a buffer between them and others, who may not appreciate their potential. One of the greatest attributes of a senior experienced leader is his/her ability to develop talent. Hopefully, the characteristics of budding leaders just described will help you to be that kind of leader.

QUESTIONS TO PONDER

Within your sphere of influence, who exhibits these characteristics?

Who have others written off because they could not see the potential within that budding leader?

Who have you written off who deserves reconsideration?

RECOMMENDED RESOURCE

Emerging Leaders: A New Breed of Church Leadership for the 21st Century (2010) by Dave Williams

INTERVIEWING (ASKING THE RIGHT QUESTIONS)

While at General Electric many years ago, I was identified as a HiPot (high potential). The practice at that time was to select HiPots and send them to GE's Leadership Development School, located in Croton on the Hudson for a week of intensive training. Young managers were invited from GE's thirteen core businesses. One hundred managers gathered and were taught key leadership practices.

One of the lessons was how to interview potential employees. Questions were presented under four categories used to assess candidates: analytical skills, accomplishments, initiative, and innovativeness (AAII). These questions have served me well over the years. I have used them repeatedly to assess potential employees. Not all the questions are asked. The interviewer selects several under each category.

These questions also can be used to prepare for an interview when you are seeking a position.

GENERAL INTERVIEW QUESTIONS

ANALYTICAL SKILLS

Typically, these will be follow-up questions to determine how the candidate thinks through and solves problems. The problems themselves are best surfaced via other lines of questioning.

- How did you approach ...?
- Were you able to foresee any of the obstacles you encountered, and if so, what did you do in anticipation of them?
- When dealing with [situation], what kinds of information did you seek? From what sources? How did you organize it?
- When planning an approach like [situation], how do you separate the important from the trivial; how do you set priorities? What kind of contingency plans do you develop (or how do you develop contingency plans)?
- When faced with a problem like [situation], what steps do you typically go through to develop an effective approach?
- Tell me about [walk me through] your thinking process as you dealt with ...

ACCOMPLISHMENTS

- When you think about some things you've done well over the last [few years/year], what are you most pleased about? Did that involve other people, or did you do it yourself? Why do you think you were able to get those results? What obstacles or problems did you overcome?
- What was it about doing . . . that gave you satisfaction? What was it that turned you on?
- How do you compare your accomplishments with those of other people in the same area [class, work group]?
- Could you describe some of the things you've done well during school as part of your regular academic program or extracurricular work? Were there obstacles, and if so, how did

you get around them? Describe the work or projects that you feel show that you know how to get the job accomplished?

- What have you learned about your strengths from working on . . .?

- Did you get any clues about your development needs because of . . .?

- Since we have only a limited amount of time to discuss your strengths, which strengths do you think stand out?

- Why do you believe you've been able to be effective; what personal characteristics/skills/special knowledge have/has been of value?

- How do you handle obstacles when they get in your way? Can you give me some examples of how you did it?

- For each of the important pieces of your work [of your assignment], would you highlight an activity or accomplishment that would demonstrate your ability to get a job done?

- How would other people you have worked with describe your accomplishments? How would they describe your strengths and the reasons you have been effective?

INITIATIVE

Accomplishments that resulted from initiatives generally will be salient and likely will be mentioned. Probes about how a project got started, for example, will help you get at some of this indirectly.

- Would you describe a project or activity at school or work where you were responsible for getting the ball rolling? What was the situation, what did you have to do, and how did people respond?

- Give me some examples of where you took initiative and what led you to do it.

- What kind of information do you like to have before you start on a project? What kinds of sources of such information do you find most valuable or useful?

- Can you give me an example of a project or activity where you started off by yourself because there was no other interested person or because if you didn't do it, no one else would?
- What leadership characteristics do you have? Would you describe them and give me some examples of how you have acted on them or used them? How would others perceive you in this regard?

Initiative frequently is evidenced where someone must deal with obstacles or make an extra effort to reach an objective.

- Why did you continue in the race of . . .?
- Why did you think it was important to . . .?
- What was so important about . . .?

INNOVATIVENESS

- Tell me about some of your best ideas and what stimulated them? How did you develop them, and how did you implement them?
- Tell me about something that you have taken special pleasure in developing, like a new way to do something, a change in a policy or procedure, or a better way to do anything.
- What kinds of situations prompt you to look for new approaches or better ways of doing things?
- Could you describe a situation at work or at school where you took a risk? What prompted you to take the risk, and how did you evaluate it ahead of time?
- Can you give me some examples of risks you have taken and why you took them? Describe the outcomes.
- Under what conditions do you take risks in an organizational setting? What was the biggest such risk you took in the past year or two, and what was the outcome?
- What obstacles did you encounter when you tried to improve something or do something differently? How did you deal with them?

- When is it appropriate to look for better ways of doing things?
- Are you more effective when you have a set of procedures to guide you or when you must develop your own way of doing things? Can you give me some examples of this?
- When you started . . . [or took over such and such], what kinds of changes, if any, did you feel the need to make? Why did you feel that way, and how did you go about making the changes?
- At what point do you settle for a solution instead of continuing to look for a better way?
- What kind of work environments encourage and/or discourage you from exploring new ideas or different way of doing things?

SPIRITUALLY FOCUSED INTERVIEW QUESTIONS

I have used the following questions to interview candidates for volunteer and paid ministry positions. Questions regarding theological understanding and spiritual maturation will get to the heart of their inner worlds. Whoever individuals are the core of their beings will animate and influence what they say and do.

THEOLOGICAL MATURATION

What theological system best describes where you are doctrinally—Calvinism (Reformed), Arminianism (Wesleyan), Dispensational, _____?

How would you describe your belief system—Fundamentalist, Conservative, Postmodern, Progressive, Liberal, _____?

What is the difference between the emerging and emergent movements?

What is your position on the following issues?

- Scriptural authority
- Salvation/eternal security
- Adam and Eve
- Eternal destiny
- Baptism

- The role of the church
- Homosexuality
- Abortion
- _____

Describe your worldview.

When was the last time you led someone to Christ?

SPIRITUAL MATURATION

Tell us how you came to be a follower of Christ.

What has your spiritual journey been like since then?

How do you maintain your spiritual vitality?

From which passages of scripture do you most like to teach?

What are your favorite books in the Bible? Why?

If you had to describe your life purpose, what would it be?

Who are your heroes? Why?

PERSONAL MATURATION

What are your hills?

- What are the hills you are prepared to die on?
- What are the hills you will bleed on?
- What hills aren't worth climbing?

How would you describe your wiring?
- Spiritual gifts
- Natural abilities
- Acquired skills
- Personality temperament
- Personal values
- Operational principles

How would you describe yourself—a leader who manages on occasion or a manager who leads on occasion?

How would you describe yourself in terms of the following?

- Strengths
- Limitations
- Weaknesses
- Potential

What are your developmental needs?

What is one thing most people do not know about you?

What would your greatest critic say about you?

If applicable, how would you describe your marriage, your wife, your children?

What are your personal goals?

What are the irreducible minimums a new position must have for you?

LEADERSHIP

Walk us through your process of the following:

- Resolving a conflict
- Solving a problem
- Recruiting volunteers
- Developing leaders

How do you prefer to be led?

What is your theory/approach to developing leaders?

What is your theory/approach to developing followers of Christ?

How do you motivate/empower others?

What is your leadership style?

- Director/coach/partner/mentor
- Commander/motivator/participator/delegator
- Primary: vision/passion/mission
- Secondary: corporate/catalytic/causal
- Team: strategic/tactical/logistical

How do you identify budding leaders?

PROFESSIONAL

What networks are you associated with?

How do you stay current?

Who is mentoring you?

Who are you mentoring?

Describe how you prepare the following:

- A presentation
- A biblical lesson
- A sermon
- A meeting
- A retreat
- An event

Tell us what you know about the 4–14 window.

What is your philosophy of ministry to young people?

What do you feel are the most critical issues facing young people today?

Why should we hire you?

If you were selected for leadership in _____, what would you emphasize?

ORIGINATION

Why do you believe you've been effective?

What personal characteristics/skills/special knowledge has been of particular value?

How do you handle obstacles when they get in your way? Can you give me some examples of how you did it?

How would other people you have worked with describe your accomplishments?

How would they describe your strengths and the reasons you have been effective?

What kind of information do you like to have before you start on a project?

What kinds of sources of such information do you find most valuable or useful?

What is the most innovative thing you have done?

I hope you find these questions helpful as you hone your interviewing technique.

QUESTIONS TO PONDER

What questions would you add to those listed above?

How will this skill change the way you conduct interviews?

How would you respond to these questions?

RECOMMENDED RESOURCE

Successful Interviewing and Recruitment: Structure the Interview; Identify Exceptional Candidates; Hire the Best Person for the Job (2010) by Rob Yeung

PROFILING (HOW TO LEVERAGE TEMPERAMENT AND LEADERSHIP STYLE)

All individuals have a unique profile that expresses who they are and the methods they prefer in exerting influence. The first is their personality temperament, and the second is their leadership style. Why be concerned about these matters? I offer the following reasons:

- To know yourself and know others
- To improve relational dynamics
- To improve communication
- To appreciate the value of others
- To be more effective as leaders
- To avoid misunderstandings
- To determine individual motivations
- To manage God's precious resources

PERSONALITY TEMPERAMENT

What is a temperament? A temperament is a set of characteristics or habitual inclinations or a predisposed emotional response that represents a personal pattern for interaction and reaction.[107]

I have read many books about personality temperament. I recognized a pattern in all the approached presented. There are essentially four basic patterns, which I have labeled A, B, C, and D for ease of identification. The chart below is a composite matrix of my findings in the books I have read.

TEMPERAMENT MATRIX
A Composite View from Many Sources
Dr. Greg Bourgond

CATEGORY	TYPE 'A'	TYPE 'B'	TYPE 'C'	TYPE 'D'
PERSONALITY STYLE	Driver, Lion, Choleric, Doer, "D"	Expressive, Otter, Sanguine, Influencer, "I"	Amiable, Golden Retriever, Phlegmatic, Relater, "S"	Analytical, Beaver, Melancholy, Thinker, "C"
	INTP-ENTP-INTJ-ENTJ	ISTP-ESTP-ISFP-ESFP	ISFJ-ESFJ-ISTJ-ESTJ	INFJ-ENFJ-INFP-ENFP
LEADERSHIP STRENGTH	Doing the Difficult	Influencing Others	Implementing Teamwork	Insuring Quality
PERSONAL MOTIVATION	Challenge Results	Recognition Desire to Help Others	Appreciation Relationships	To Be Right Quality
LEADS THROUGH	Forcefulness Persistence	Verbal Skills Motivational Skills	Building Relationships Group Interaction	Structure Methodology
LEADERSHIP WEAKNESS	Insensitive Impatient Inflexible Demanding Taking On Too Much	Impulsive Too Optimistic Lack of Follow Through Talking Too Much Jumping To Conclusions	Non-Initiating Resists Change Avoids Conflict Being Indecisive Meeting Deadlines	Overly Cautious Too Detailed Pessimistic Rigidness Resisting Responsibility
UNDER TENSION	Autocratic	Attacks	Acquiesces	Avoids
NEEDS TO TRUST GOD FOR	Unconditional Love Patience with Others Being More Flexible	Better Control of Time Discipline Discernment	More Goal Orientation Facing Confrontation Initiating More	Being More Optimistic Self-Confidence Being More Open
NEEDS OTHERS TO PROVIDE	Sensitivity to Others Caution Details and Facts	To Handle Details A Logical Approach Concentration on Task	Stretch to Challenge Help Solving Problems Initiative and Change	Quick Decision Making Reassurance Stretching of Capabilities
IDEAL LEADERSHIP SITUATION	Challenge Change Freedom Authority	New and Exciting Freedom from Detail Opportunity to Motivate Social Interaction	Area of Specialization Working with a Group Consistency Opportunity to Help	Clearly Defined Requires Precision Limited Risk Methodology & Structure
IMPROVEMENT AREA	Listening	Pausing	Initiating More	Declaring
BIBLICAL MODELS	Paul & Martha	Peter & Ruth	Barnabas & Mary	Moses & Mary (Jesus)

By reviewing the matrix, you will undoubtedly think that you have a mixture of characteristics in one or more of the four categories. I would suggest you are more one type than the others, even though some of the characteristics may fall in the other categories.

When God formed you in your mother's womb, he determined the temperament you would possess. Knowing your temperament will help you understand why you respond to a given situation the way you do

---

[107] Adapted from *Webster's Ninth New Collegiate Dictionary*.

and why you may see things differently from someone else. Knowing others' temperaments will help you understand why they respond the way they do. It will result in better communication as well.

By referring to the chart below, what temperament is most true about you? Notice the correlation as well with other temperament schemes. The matrix will also help you determine your leadership strengths, your personal motivation, how you lead most effectively, your leadership weaknesses, how you respond under tension, what you need to trust God for, what you need others to provide, what the characteristics and an ideal leadership situation look like, your major need of improvement, and biblical models who represent each of the styles.

LEADERSHIP STYLE

What is a leadership style? One's leadership style refers to the individual behaviors a leader utilizes to function in his/her leadership role to influence followers. This includes categories such as how the leader motivates or relates to followers, how followers perceive the leader in the leader's role, and how the leader solves group problems, attempts to bring about obedience among followers, and resolves differences.

This individual expression includes the following:

- Methodology for handling crises
- Methodology for problem solving
- Methodology for decision-making
- Relationships to peers and followers
- Persuasion techniques for exerting shades of influence on others

What is the difference between personality temperaments and leadership styles? Our personality temperament is our expression of being. Our leadership style is our method of influence.

Paul Hersey identified four types of leaders: director (S1), coach (S2), partner-supporter (S3), and mentor-observer (S4).[108] A detailed description of these styles can be found in the chapter titled "Motivating."

Both Erwin McManus, lead pastor of Mosaic in Los Angeles, and J. Robert Clinton, former professor of leadership at Fuller Seminary, have done considerable research on leadership styles. I will simply state them for you.

LEADERSHIP STYLES—ERWIN MCMANUS

In McManus's scheme, he identifies primary, secondary, and team leadership styles. The primary leadership styles include vision, passion, and mission. The secondary leadership styles include corporate, catalytic, and causal. Finally, team leadership styles include strategic, tactical, and logistical leaders.

Regarding primary leadership styles, descriptions for each are as follows:

- *Vision*: Envisions clearly God's future—clarity. Defines the focus (purpose, aim) of what we do and answers the question of why. Responsible for commission. Sees possibilities and solves problems. Sees out two years or more. Visionary leaders (theorists) draw strategic personnel who may be catalytic or corporate leaders. Solomon and John would be examples of this category.

- *Passion*: Experiences deeply God's concerns—intensity. Defines the form (style, pattern) of what we do and answers the question of how. Responsible for community. Coaches and counsels. Sees out thirty days. Passionate leaders (zealots) draw tactical personnel who may be catalytic or causal leaders. Elisha and Peter would be examples of this category.

- *Mission*: Embraces personally God's appointment—destiny. Defines the scope (task, ministry) of what we do and answers the

108   Paul Hersey, *The Situational Leader* (Escondido: Center for Leadership Studies, 1997), 36–39.

question of what. Responsible for communication. Coordinates and organizes. Sees out one day. Mission leaders (specialists) draw logistical personnel who may be corporate or causal leaders. Noah and Luke would be examples of this category.

Regarding secondary leadership styles, Erwin describes them as follows:

- *Corporate leaders*: They bring together the powerful focus and intentionality of vision and mission. Corporate leaders are visionary strategists who are best suited to working with systems and structures. Through their ability to invest in long-term goals and to use organizational structures to accomplish them, they often emerge as both entrepreneurs and executive leaders. Nehemiah and James would be examples of this style.

These persons must ensure that they are constantly in touch with the emotional transitioning of people and not simply the restructuring of the organization. The human factor is often the missing link and the Achilles' heel of their leadership. These leaders must surround themselves with the counselors who have their hands on the pulse of the people. They will increase their effectiveness by remembering that people are motivated by passion.

- *Catalytic leaders*: They bring together the dynamic and catalytic combination of vision and passion. They are entrepreneurial initiators who work best in an environment in which they can generate new ideas and new actions. They are natural risk takers who test boundaries and barriers. They often emerge as new paradigm pioneers. David and Apollos would be examples of this style.

These individuals must ensure that they are continually identifying and developing emerging leadership, as they rarely remain in whatever endeavor they have initiated. They must choose either to establish a long–term base of ministry or unify their ministries through a common purpose or mission. Without a commitment to reproduce and restrict themselves, their efforts may be diluted and fail to result in a multigenerational impact.

- *Causal leaders*: They bring together the persuasive and focused intensity of passion and mission. They are compelling flag-bearers for the causes they care deeply about. They work best on short time assignments that require rapid mobilization and response. Excelling under pressure, they often emerge as exceptional cause-and-crisis leadership. Elijah and Stephen would be examples of this style.

These individuals must ensure they are connected continually to a visionary. Otherwise, they may focus too much on short-term issues that are disconnected from the long-term goals of the ministry. Driven by values and issues, they lead others through hands-on activism. They will increase their effectiveness in decision-making by beginning with the end in mind.

Regarding team leadership styles, dream-team excellence needs strategic personnel, tactical personnel, and logistical personnel, according to Erwin.

- *Strategic leaders*: Skillful development, coordination, and employment of goals and tactics. Set challenging visionary goals that often seem impossible to achieve. They are analytical and systematic in their thinking and are gifted in the ability to foresee the implications of present decisions on future effectiveness. Strategic leaders are two-year visionaries. Their spiritual-gift mix may include faith, leadership, apostleship, discernment, or words of wisdom.
- *Tactical leaders*: Expeditious implementation of task. Develop objectives to accomplish goals. Tactical personnel are powerful motivators with the uncanny ability to mobilize others to accomplish a specific task. They will ensure the implementation

and application of theory and will drive impersonal concepts to the meeting of human needs. They are players/coaches who believe deeply in their causes and care deeply for their teams. They are hands-on leaders who are highly focused on the task at hand. Tactical leaders are thirty-day visionaries. They excel in short-term projects. Their spiritual-gift mix might include exhortation, helps, mercy, hospitality, or prophecy.

- *Logistical leaders*: Streamline organization and administration related to the mobilization of resources, materials, and information. Logistical personnel will ensure the simplification of abstract concepts, provide the factual and data validation to the intuitive leaps, and manage the organization of material. Logistical leaders are one-day visionaries. They administrate the immediate next step in the overall strategy. Their spiritual-gift mix might include administration, serving, giving, word of knowledge, or teaching.

LEADERSHIP STYLES—DR. J. ROBERT CLINTON

"At the heart of leadership style theory is the way the leader operates towards followers in all that he/she does. These behaviors are usually located upon a continuum characterized by four basic positions; highly directive, directive, non-directive and highly non-directive." [109] In Dr. Clinton's words, each category is described as follows:

Commander—highly directive: Leader makes decisions. Leader gives specific instructions, closely supervises carrying out instructions, and feels a need to personally control.

- *Apostolic style:* The leader assumes the role of delegated authority or those for whom he/she is responsible, receives revelation from God concerning decisions, and commands obedience based on

---

[109] J. Robert Clinton, *Leaders, Leadership and the Bible* (Altadena: Barnabas Publishers, 1993), 43–53.

the role of delegated authority and revelation concerning God's will.[110]

- *Confrontation style:* An approach to problem solving that brings the problem out in the open with all parties concerned, that analyzes the problem considering revelational truth, and that brings force to bear upon the parties to accept recommended solutions.[111]

- *Father-initiator style:* Similar to the apostolic style and uses the leverage that comes to those who have founded the work for getting acceptance of influence. Obligation is used as a power base.[112]

Motivator—directive: Leader makes decisions, may dialogue, may explain. Demands feedback, intervenes frequently to ensure results, feels responsible for implementing, and has a need to control.

- *Obligation/persuasion style:* Refers to an appeal for followers to obey some recommended directives that persuade, not command followers heed some advice. It leaves the decision to do so in the hands of the followers but forces the followers to recognize their obligations to the leader, due to past service by the leader to the follower. Strongly implies that the follower owes the leader some debt and should follow the recommended advice as part of paying back the obligation. Finally, it reflects the leader's strong expectation that the follower will conform to the persuasive advice.[113]

- *Father/guardian style:* This style has as its major concern protection and encouragement for followers. Expresses a caring relationship between the leader and the follower. Often

---

[110] 1 Thessalonians 2:6; 5:12–13; 1 Timothy 5:17; Hebrews 13:7.
[111] Corinthian letters and Jude.
[112] 1 Corinthians 4:14–15.
[113] Philemon and 1 and 2 Corinthians.

used when the leader is spiritually mature, and followers are spiritually immature.[114]

Participator—nondirective: Leader and followers decide; leader shares ideas and facilitates and encourages follower-made decisions with guidance and encouragement. Leader monitors, gives guidance only when needed; follower gives frequent feedback; follower feels responsible for implementing results.

- *Maturity appeal style:* A form of leadership influence that counts upon godly experience, usually gained over a long period of time; an empathetic identification based on a common sharing of experience; and a recognition of the force of imitation modeling in influencing people to convince people toward a favorable acceptance of the leader's ideas.[115]
- *Nurse style:* A behavior style characterized by gentleness and sacrificial service and loving care, which indicates that a leader has given up rights in order not to impede the nurture of those following him/her.[116]

Delegator—highly nondirective: Follower makes decisions and is responsible for the decision and may keep leader informed. Leader observes; intervenes only for corrective feedback, while the follower feels responsible for implementing the results.

- *Imitator style:* Refers to a conscious use of imitation modeling as a means for influencing followers. The user models appropriate thinking or behavior, with an expectant view that followers must, will, and should be encouraged to follow his/her example.[117]
- *Consensus style:* Refers to the approach to leadership influence that involves the group itself actively participating in

---

[114] 1 Thessalonians 2:10–11.
[115] 1 Peter 5:1–4; 2 John; 3 John; 2 Corinthians 11:16–33; 12:1–10.
[116] 1 Thessalonians 2:7; 2 Timothy 2:24–25.
[117] Philippians 4:9; 2 Timothy 3:10–11.

decision-making and coming to solutions acceptable to the whole group. The leader must be skilled in bringing diverse thoughts together in such a way as to meet the whole group needs.[118]

- *Indirect conflict style:* An approach to problem solving that requires discernment of spiritual motivation factors behind the problem; usually results in spiritual motivation factors behind the problem; usually results in spiritual warfare without direct confrontation with the parties of the problem.[119]

Knowing your personality temperament and leadership style will help you leverage your influence and effectiveness for God's redemptive purposes.

QUESTIONS TO PONDER

What is your and your team's personality temperament and leadership style?

What is your family's personality temperament and leadership style?

How will this affect how you will lead going forward?

RECOMMENDED RESOURCE

Discovering Your Leadership Style: The Power of Chemistry, Strategy and Spirituality (2014) by David T. Olson

---

[118] Acts 5; 13, and 15.

[119] 1 Corinthians 5: 3–5; Matthew 16:21–23; Mark 3: 20–30; Ephesians 6:10–20.

DEVELOPING (HOW TO DEVELOP AND TRAIN LEADERS)

Lovett H. Weems, president of Saint Paul School of Theology in Kansas City, Missouri, observed that leadership studies over the past fifty years have identified at least 350 definitions for leadership. James McGregor Burns commented that leadership is the most observed and least understood phenomenon on earth.

Leadership has been defined as follows:

> General Charles Gordon once asked Li Hung Chang, an old Chinese leader, "What is leadership?" He replied, "There are only three kinds of people in the world—those that are immovable, those that are moveable, and those that move them."[120]

Walter C. Wright Jr. suggests that leadership is a relationship in which one person seeks to influence the behaviors, beliefs, attitudes, or values of another. In the context of organizational management,

---

[120]   Leighton Ford, *Transforming Leadership: Jesus' Way of Creating Vision, Shaping Values & Empowering Change* (Downers Grove: InterVarsity Press, 1991), 91.

leadership is a relationship of influence with the twin objectives of accomplishing a task and developing the people.

Norman Shawchuck, an international leadership and management consultant, said leadership is the ability and the activity of influencing people and of shaping their behavior.

According to Joel Barker, the originator of the often-used phrase "paradigm shift," a leader is someone you will follow to a place you wouldn't go by yourself. David Cook and Howard Hendricks offer their own definition: A leader is a person who influences people to accomplish a purpose.

In my opinion, Dr. J. Robert Clinton (1989), former professor of leadership for the School of World Mission of Fuller Theological Seminary, does the best job of defining leadership and a leader from a biblical point of view. For me, his definition of a leader captures the significance of being God's leader. He defines leadership and a leader as follows:

> Leadership is a dynamic process over an extended period of time in various situations in which a leader utilizing leadership resources and by specific leadership behaviors, influences the thoughts and activities of followers toward accomplishment of aims usually mutually beneficial for leaders, followers, and the macro context of which they are a part. A leader is a person with a God-given capacity and a God-given responsibility to influence a specific group of God's people toward his purposes for the group.[121]

Have you ever tried to make sense of the individual incidents of your life? We pour over these events, trying to unlock the mystery of their purpose. When clear answers aren't forthcoming, we begin to form

---

[121] J. Robert Clinton, *Leadership Emergence Theory: A Self-Study Manual for Analyzing the Development of a Christian Leader* (Altadena: Barnabas Publishers, 1989), 36, 40.

theories that provide a rational answer. We certainly understand, at least intellectually, "that in all things God works for the good of those who love him, who have been called according to his purpose."[122] Have you ever considered that some events do not have a specific purpose in and of themselves, that they are part of a larger plan of God in accordance with his purposes? He may not initiate every situation we face or event we experience, but he uses these incidents to shape us as his leaders. The pattern of development becomes clear only over time. In retrospect and in the power of his Spirit, we look over the topography of our lives and see the unmistakable pattern of his activity emerge.

For many years, Dr. J. Robert Clinton has studied the lives of over 3,800 Christian leaders—biblical, historical, and contemporary leaders. He has taken seriously the admonition of the writer of Hebrews, who said,

> Remember your former leaders who spoke God's message to you. Think back on how they lived and died and imitate their faith. Jesus Christ is the same yesterday, today and forever. (Hebrews 13:7–8)

His extensive research has been popularized in his book *The Making of a Leader*, first published in 1988 and updated in 2012.[123] Bobby Clinton, as he prefers to be called, has produced a significant body of research about leadership from a biblical and theological perspective. *The Making of a Leader* is only the tip of the iceberg. A more detailed description of leadership emergence theory can be explored in the reference manual *Leadership Emergence Theory* (1989).[124]

One overarching question motivated his research on the topic of leadership development: "Does God develop a leader according to a

---

[122] Romans 8:29.

[123] J. Robert Clinton, *The Making of a Leader: Recognizing the Lessons and Stages of Leadership Development* (Colorado Springs: NavPress, 2012).

[124] J. Robert Clinton, *Leadership Emergence Theory—A Self-Study Manual for Analyzing the Development of a Christian Leader* (Altadena: Barnabas Publishers, 1989).

divine pattern?" The results of his research, and that of his students, have produced a body of literature on the subject that is second to none.

Bobby Clinton has concluded that God indeed takes an active role in the development of his leaders. He contends that leaders are shaped in accordance with specific patterns and processes over the course of our lifetime. Development, he says, includes all life's processes, not just formal training. In general, he has learned three important facts. In his own words, let me state them for you.

1. A Christian leader is a person with a God-given capacity and a God-given responsibility, who influences a specific group of God's people toward God's purposes. We explored this definition earlier.
2. Leadership emergence is a process in which God intervenes throughout a lifetime in crucial ways to shape that leader toward God's purposes for that leader.
3. When viewed from a whole-life perspective, God's intervention or shaping is intentional. his processing is intended to develop the leader's capacity. It moves the leader to operate at realized potential in terms of giftedness; that is, natural abilities, acquired skills, and spiritual gifts.

Bobby Clinton goes on to say, however, that God's intentional shaping also allows for a given leader's response to that shaping. In other words, leadership development can be thwarted or enhanced by the developing leader's response to God's shaping.

Broadly speaking, a leader's development hinges around three major variables: processing, time, and response. The goals of development include spiritual formation with a focus on leadership character, ministerial formation with a focus on leadership skills, and strategic formation with a focus on ministry philosophy. Ministry philosophy, according to Bobby's definition, is an integrated set of leadership values.

During his research, Bobby Clinton has identified six phases of leadership development:

- Phase I: sovereign foundations
- Phase II: inner-life growth
- Phase III: ministry maturing
- Phase IV: life maturing
- Phase V: convergence
- Phase VI: afterglow

In the first three phases, God is primarily working *in* the leader. In the last three phases, God is working *through* the leader. In any case, we need to remember that we minister out of what we are. God is concerned with what we are, not with what we accomplish. Leadership is an inside-out process. A survey of books about leadership would reveal that most deal with leadership skills. Lately, more books are being written on the character, or being, of the leader, no doubt stimulated by the debate raging today around this issue.

Let me reframe the subject by saying I can teach anyone leadership skills. It is true that those who are born leaders lead intuitively. I find it interesting that when intuitive leaders are asked to describe their leadership methodology, they find it hard to delineate the skills they use without thinking. Regarding those of us who are not born leaders, our capacity for leadership is only limited by our aptitude, maturity, and discipline. Timothy, as far as we can tell, did not have the gift of evangelism. Yet Paul, his mentor, told him to do the work of an evangelist. You may not have the gift of leadership, but you are to do the work of a leader.

Back to the issue at hand. Effective godly leadership is foremost a matter of character and secondarily a matter of skill. God is interested in the heart of the leader, as evidenced by his response to Samuel's confusion regarding the qualities of Israel's next king. "Do not consider his appearance or his height, for I have rejected him. The LORD does not look at the things man looks at. Man looks at the outward appearance, but the LORD looks at the heart" (1 Samuel 16:7).

So how does God develop his leaders? According to Dr. Clinton, the process begins with preconversion development called *sovereign foundations*. Clinton stresses that God providentially works foundational items into the life of the leader-to-be. Personality characteristics, experiences (good and bad), and the time context will be used by God. Character traits are embedded. This phase is preconversion.

The second phase of development, *inner-life growth*, focuses on character and skill development. The emerging leader, according to Bobby, usually receives training in this phase. Often it is informal, relating to ministry. The leader-to-be learns by doing in the context of a local church or Christian organization. Learning generally takes place through imitation modeling, informal apprenticeships, and mentoring. This phase may also include formal training, such as Bible school or seminary. Again, ministry training and character building are the focus.

The third phase, *ministry maturing*, deals primarily with general ministry development. The emerging leader gets into ministry as a prime focus of life. He or she will get further training—informally, through self-study or growth projects; or nonformally, through functionally oriented workshops and/or seminars. Major activities are ministry-related. The training that goes on is incidental to the ministry process.

In the fourth phase, called *life maturing*, the emphasis is on personal ministry development. The leader begins to use his or her gift mix with power. There is mature fruitfulness. God is working through the leader to influence others. This is a period in which giftedness emerges along with priorities. This phase is marked by a growing awareness and confidence with one's identity. God's wiring becomes very clear. Leaders know what they are good at and not good at. They gravitate to those ministry opportunities that allow full expression of who they are.

It is in the fifth phase that God is directing the leader. Clinton calls this phase *convergence*, or personally focused ministry. According to Bobby Clinton, the leader is moved by God into a role that matches gift mix, experience, temperament, passion, and vision. This phase frees the leader from ministry for which there is no gift and enhances and uses the best that the leader has to offer. Not many leaders experience convergence. Often, they are promoted to roles that hinder their gift mix. In convergence, being and spiritual authority form the true power base for mature ministry. If leaders reach convergence, they find complete fulfillment because they, in effect, begin to realize their full created

DR. GREGORY W. BOURGOND

potential. I describe this phase this way—when 80 percent of who you are, how God has wired you, matches 80 percent of what you do.

The last phase is called celebration or *afterglow*, in which the leader experiences wide ministry influence. According to Clinton, for a very few the fruit of a lifetime of ministry and growth culminates in an era of recognition and indirect influence at broad levels. Leaders in this phase have built up a lifetime of contacts and continue to exert influence in these relationships. Others will seek them out because of their consistent track record in following God. As Clinton indicates, the influence of the leader at this point is more indirect than direct. The character and ministry of the leader speaks so loudly that it cannot help but influence others outside the immediate sphere of influence of that leader. For example, Billy Graham has (and Bill Breight had) amazing influence on people who have never met them personally. The model of their lives serves as a living testimony that results in admiration and respect of countless others.

Let's look more closely at Clinton's leadership dynamics, including development pattern, process items, boundary events, and sphere of influence.

Regarding the development pattern arising from the study of Christian leaders, Clinton concludes that God develops a leader over a lifetime. That development is a function of the use of events and people to impress leadership lessons upon a leader (called processing), time, and the leader's response to these lessons. Bobby stresses the fact that all leaders can point to critical incidents in their lives when God taught them something very important.

Clinton identifies over fifty process items God uses to shape a leader. Process items deal with the ways and means used by God to move a leader along the overall pattern of development. The chiseling tools God may use include providential events, people, circumstances, interventions, and inner-life lessons.

For our purposes, I will describe four process items God uses to shape a leader: integrity checks, obedience checks, word checks, and ministry tasks.

An *integrity check* is a test that God uses to evaluate intentions to shape character. This test is a springboard to an expanded sphere of influence. It consists of a challenge to consistency with inner convictions and the response to the challenge. If the leader successfully responds to these checks, he or she can expect an expansion of ministry.

For example, in Daniel 1:8–21, Daniel resolved not to defile himself with royal food and wine. He knew defiance of the king could mean the loss of his life and that of his companions. He stood his ground, and God honored him as a result.

What integrity checks have you experienced lately? How did you do?

An *obedience check* is a process item through which a leader learns to recognize, understand, and obey God's voice. Through it, God tests a leader's personal response to revealed truth. Many are called to lay something on the altar; and they do, but they take along a rubber knife. Our obedience, at times, is not complete; some strings are attached.

Abraham underwent an obedience check when, in Genesis 22:1–2 and Hebrews 11:17–19, we are told he was commanded to take his son, Isaac, whom he loved, and sacrifice him as a burnt offering. As you recall, Abraham responded with obedience. How would you have responded?

What obedience checks have you experienced lately? How did you do?

A *word check* tests a leader's ability to understand or receive a word from God personally and then allow God to work it out in his/her life. Successfully passing a word check will lead to more revealed truth. The right to influence comes from the ability to clarify God's truth to others.

Samuel, the judge and prophet, heard the voice of God and responded by saying, "Speak Lord, for your servant is listening." When is the last time you heard the still small voice of God?[125] When is the last time you really listened?

What word checks have you experienced lately? How did you respond?

The last process item I want to mention is *ministry tasks*. A ministry task, according to Clinton, "is an assignment from God that tests a

---

[125]   1 Samuel 3:1–10.

person's faithfulness and obedience to use his or her gifts in a task that has a beginning and ending, accountability, and evaluation." A ministry challenge is the means through which a leader is prompted by God to sense the need for and accept a new assignment. A ministry task may include calls to do something, serve in some way, help someone, lead something, do something, resolve something, organize something, or plan something.

Paul, then known as Saul, and Barnabas were set apart by the Spirit of God for a work ordained by the Spirit.[126] This work would he would be used of God with his skills would be honed as he ministered.

What ministry tasks have you been assigned, or have you rejected lately? How did they or are they shaping your ministry skills?

Let's turn to another of Clinton's constructs—boundary events (see chapter on Transitioning). Boundary events bring about a shift from one phase of leadership development to the next. Such events may include crises, promotions, a new ministry, learning a major new concept, having an unusual experience, life-changing encounters with a person, a divine guidance experience, or a geographic move.

In retrospect, as you reflect over the past, what boundary events have served to usher you into a new phase of leadership development? At the time, you may not have recognized the significance, but now you see God's hand in it.

Finally, let's look at sphere of influence. Each of us, as leaders, has been given a sphere of influence by God, a ministry area or group of people to whom we are called to serve and for whom the leader will give an account to God. As we progress in our development as leaders under the hand of God, our sphere of influence increases. A change in our sphere of influence usually signals a change in development phases.

The type of influence may change as well. In the initial phases of development, our direct influence will increase as we mature as leaders. In the latter phases, our indirect influence grows at a greater rate. Those to whom we minister directly are, in turn, ministering to many others who don't know us directly. Also, to the degree we have opportunity and

---

[126] Acts 13:1–3.

skill, our writings impact others we have not met. For me, personally, several historical mentors whom I have not met have had significant influence on me. They include A. W. Tozer; G. Campbell Morgan; D. Martyn Lloyd-Jones; my contemporary mentor, J. R. Clinton (as is plainly evident); Vance Havner, whom I had the occasion to meet just before his death; and others.

Who has had a significant positive influence on your life whom you have not met personally but have benefitted from his/her ministry?

Can you describe the sphere of influence you have been given by God and for whom you will give an account?

In summary, different kinds of process items occur to help us move along the development timeline. Each phase is terminated by a boundary event precipitated by successfully navigating through the process items. With each progressive phase, the leader's sphere of influence increases in size and/or responsibility, both directly and indirectly.

Given the information I have shared, where would you place yourself on J. Robert Clinton's leadership development timeline? Take some time to reflect on how God has developed you to date.

As a gentle warning, we can interrupt God's development plans for us by refusing to effectively respond to his process items. Let me close by suggesting seven barriers to healthy leadership development, first presented in a retreat setting by Dr. Jerry Sheveland when he was senior pastor of College Avenue Baptist Church in San Diego. His text for the message was 1 Peter 5:2–11.

Leadership development in our lives will be adversely affected and impacted when the following occurs:

1. A grudging spirit begins to replace a willing spirit. Be shepherds of God's flock that is under your care, serving as overseer—not because you must but because you are willing (1 Peter 5:2a).
2. Material desires begin to overwhelm ministry desires. God wants you to be not greedy for money but eager to serve (1 Peter 5:2).

3. Manipulation becomes a substitute for mentoring. Do not lord it over those entrusted to you but be an example to the flock (1 Peter 5:3).

4. Short-term goals prevail over eternal goals. And when the Chief Shepherd appears, you will receive the crown of glory that will never fade away (1 Peter 5:4).

5. Ambition begins to undermine humility. Young men, in the same way, be submissive to those who are older. All of you, clothe yourselves with humility toward one another because "God opposes the proud but gives grace to the humble." Humble yourselves, therefore, under God's mighty hand, that he may lift you up in due time (1 Peter 5:5–6).

6. Anxiety begins to compromise faith. Cast all your anxiety on him because he cares for you (1 Peter 5:7).

7. Spiritual carelessness begins to erode spiritual discipline. Be self-controlled and alert. Your enemy, the devil, prowls around like a roaring lion, looking for someone to devour. Resist him, standing firm in the faith, because you know that your brothers throughout the world are undergoing the same kind of sufferings. And the God of all grace, who called you to his eternal glory in Christ, after you have suffered a little while, will himself restore you and make you strong, firm, and steadfast. To him be the power for ever and ever. Amen (1 Peter 5:8–11).

These seven barriers will produce atrophy in the development of a leader.

TRAINING FRAMEWORK

In a video titled *Developing Leaders for Ministry*, George Barna, president of the Barna Research Group, cited ten essential suggestions for developing leaders, gleaned from analysis of churches committed to that mission.

1. Subject every candidate to thorough assessment.

2. Create a customized development plan. Recognize that people learn differently.
3. Provide each leader with a mentor or coach.
4. Give developing leaders ample access to the directing leader.
5. Provide some formal classroom instruction.
6. Facilitate significant peer interaction.
7. Institute an aggressive program of access to leadership resources.
8. Establish adequate intercessory prayer support.
9. Allow developing leaders to have progressive leadership experiences.
10. Implement a reasonable accountability process.

Christian leaders are far more interested in being trained by their churches than other organizations. Every leader has a dominant aptitude for leadership (e.g., directing leader, strategic leader, team-building leaders, or operational leader).

So where should a training program focus? I am familiar with too many leadership programs that focus their development on building competencies. Leaders are much more than the competencies they possess. Who leaders are at the core will inform and condition what they do, how they do it, and the degree of effectiveness and efficiency they will enjoy doing it. Knowing what to do and what can be done effectively and efficiently will depend on the awareness leaders have regarding their unique God-ordained wiring. Therefore, several spheres of engagement, in my view, are warranted.

Leader Development Spheres

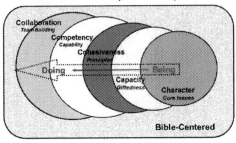

Dr. Greg Bourgond © 2001

Character deals with the core issues of beliefs, values, attitudes, and motives. *Capacity* addresses spiritual gifts, talents, strengths, leadership style, and personality temperament. *Cohesiveness* explores principles and focal issues leading to focused leadership. *Competency* identifies key abilities required for effective leadership. *Collaboration* presents team-building exercises.

In my experience, any leadership development training must address three major areas: leadership character, leadership competence, and leadership congruence.

The first, leadership character, seeks to tune the leader's heart to the heart of God by addressing and informing central beliefs, core values, a biblical worldview, and primary motives compelling God-honoring behavior.

The second, leadership competence, should address the competencies that can be applied in any setting, as well as tasks specific to the role they will assume. At least three areas of development should be considered: development, planning, and engagement competencies.

Any program of development should include development competencies, such as personal soul care, personal management, recruiting of emerging leaders,[127] measuring leadership, mentoring, motivation and empowerment, and team building.

---

[127] See chapter "Recruiting" for clarification regarding budding or emerging leaders and what features characterize them.

In addition, planning competencies such as cultural exegesis, visioning, communication, ministry planning, systems understanding, organizing, resourcing and networking, monitoring, and evaluation should be addressed.

Finally, engagement competencies such as transformational leadership, leading and managing, power bases and influence, decision-making and problem solving, conflict resolution, and effecting change would be helpful in the development of leaders.

Leadership congruence helps leaders get in touch with how God has wired them uniquely and how that wiring can be leveraged to facilitate God's redemptive purposes in a fallen world. Determining one's biblical purpose, life purpose, committed passion, role nonnegotiables, unique methodologies (personal tool kit), and ultimate contribution can be a powerful motivation to move from shotgun to laser beam in terms of engagement of ministry opportunities.

Requiring deliverables for character, competence, and congruence phases will help solidify lessons learned. For instance, requiring an action plan for character development at the end of leadership character training would personalize what has been learned by the trainee. Requiring development of a giftedness and leader profile unique to that leader for the competence phase will inform how he/she uses the tools God has given him/her. A personal life mandate and lifelong learning plan for the congruence phase will help leaders bring focus and intentionality to their ministry roles.

One last thought—in developing a leadership development program consider the following:

- Provide general training as described above and tailor training for specific roles.
- Make use of available resources (e.g., books, manuals, workshops, seminars, classes, courses, inventories, assessment instruments, online resources, etc.).
- Provide several formats for training, such as classroom, online, mentoring, team-building exercises, apprenticeships,

internships, shadowing, ministry experience, and exposure to accomplished leaders.

- Provide ongoing training for core leaders specific to their needs for development. This training should address both corrective and preventive development.
- Continually conduct formative (in situ) and summative evaluation of your leadership development program to update and revise your training initiatives.
- Appoint a champion to lead the leadership development process and provide the resources, personnel, and budget necessary for successful implementation and ongoing conduct.
- Infuse the development process with the DNA of your church or ministry organization (mission, vision, beliefs, values, objectives, and strategies) to ensure the leaders reflect interests of the church.

In closing, be aware of God's intentionality in your development as a leader. Be aware of the process items he uses to shape his leaders. Understand that we all make mistakes, that God is a God of the second chance, that we are in the process of becoming but have not yet arrived. He is not finished with you and me. Submit to his shaping influence over your life. God has plans for you!

QUESTIONS TO PONDER

How do you identify, recruit, train, and evaluate leaders?

What would comprise a leadership development program for your setting?

What resources would you recommend for developing leaders?

RECOMMENDED RESOURCE

Building Leaders: Blueprints for Developing Leadership at Every Level of Your Church (2004) by Aubrey Malphurs

MENTORING (HOW TO MENTOR AND BE MENTORED)

The journey that leads to finishing well requires guides to help reach our desired destination. We cannot journey alone. We need others to help along the way. Research has indicated several characteristics of those who finished well. Those who finished well had a network of meaningful relationships and as many as ten to fifteen important mentors during their lifetimes.

Mentoring has long been a strategy to pass on to others what is learned and has been learned on the journey. Mentoring is a relational experience in which one person empowers another by sharing God-given resources.

Words like mentor, mentoree, and mentoring can conjure up various meanings for each of us. For some, the words evoke memories of positive, life-changing relationships; for others, the words remind them of a yearning for something they know they need in their development as a person, a professional, a Christian, or even as a leader but have yet to find such a person.

Where did the term *mentor* originate? In *The Iliad*, Odysseus, better known as Ulysses by the Romans much later, contracts Mentor, his "wise and trusted counselor," as a tutor for his son, Telemachus, before leaving on a long journey that lasted twenty years. This journey was precipitated by the kidnapping of Helen by Paris, the son of the king of Troy. Mentor's name—with a lower case *m*—has passed into our language as a shorthand term for wise and trusted counselor and teacher.

A mentor is a person with a serving, giving, encouraging attitude who sees leadership potential in a younger leader and can promote or otherwise significantly influence that younger leader along to the realization of his or her potential. A mentoree or protégé is a person who receives empowerment in the mentoring relationship. Mentoring is a relational process; the mentor is one who knows or has experienced something and transfers that something (resources of wisdom, information, experience, confidence, insight, relationships, status, etc.) to a mentoree at an appropriate time and manner, so that it facilitates development or empowerment.

The Bible is full of examples of mentoring: Jethro counseled Moses, Moses guided Joshua, Jonathan was a peer mentor of David, David sponsored Solomon, Solomon taught his children, Elijah advised Elisha, Jesus mentored the apostles and others, Barnabas encouraged Paul, and Paul was a spiritual guide to Timothy, Titus, and Onesimus.

Why consider mentoring?

- People are longing for their stories to be heard and their lives to be shaped. It is one of the most effective ways to change lives.
- It provides an avenue for passing on what we have learned.
- It is one of the most effective ways to shape a person's character.
- It can be a significant means to facilitate discipleship.
- It is essential to finishing well as a Christian leader.
- It reflects a primary way Jesus impacted lives and practiced ministry.

Many mentors of various kinds will be needed throughout your journey. Mentors share their God-given resources, experiences, expertise, spiritual maturity, and networks to help in your lifelong development. Intensive mentors (discipler, spiritual guide, or coach) may be needed to help develop strong faith foundations. Occasional mentors (counselor, teacher, or sponsor) may be required to help you with a specific need or in a particular area. Passive mentors (exemplary model, historical people of faith, or divine contact) may be required to build expertise or acquire new skills or feed your soul.

MENTORING CATEGORIES & TYPES		
Category	Intensive	Occasional	Passive
Process	*Formal*	*Non-formal*	*Informal*
Focus	Foundations	Needs	Inspirations
Type	Discipler Establishing basics of following Christ and the foundations of the faith	Counselor Perspective and advise for relationships and life circumstances	Divine Contact Person, word, and/or circumstances used to confirm God's direction or will
	Spiritual Guide Establishing inward, outward, and upward spiritual disciplines	Teacher Knowledge and understanding of specific topics	Contemporary Model Living model for life and ministry or exposure to teaching through books, audio, or video
	Coach Motivation, encouragement and skill development	Sponsor Career guidance, protection, networking and promotion	Historical Model Deceased model for life and ministry or exposure to teaching through books, audio, or video
SELF-EVALUATION		
What am I doing now I need to KEEP doing?		
What am I doing now I need to CHANGE?		
What am I doing now I need to STOP doing?		
What am I not doing now I need to START doing?		

The resources shared in a mentoring relationship could include wisdom and discernment, life and ministry experience, timely advice, new methods, skills, principles, important values and lessons, organizational influence, sponsorship, networking, and, on occasion, financial resources. Finding the appropriate mentor for a situation or circumstance requires prayer and thoughtful consideration.

There are five dynamics on the path to mentoring relationships. These dynamics define five aspects of mentoring:

- Attraction—like attracts like. People naturally move toward those who seem helpful. Mentorees may be attracted by a mentor's personality, spirituality, ministry skills, or experience.
- Relationship—the best exchanges of empowerment resources happen when mentors and mentorees trust each other.

- Responsiveness—the mentoree's willingness to respond to the mentor's information is vital for learning empowerment.
- Accountability—mentorees must answer to someone for their growth and spiritual development. Often there is mutual accountability between mentors and mentorees.
- Empowerment—this is the actual exchange of resources and encouragement between mentor and mentoree in areas of life and ministry.

Common characteristics mark a good mentor: ability to readily see potential in a person; tolerance with mistakes; brashness, abrasiveness and the like to see that potential develop; flexibility in responding to people and circumstances; patience, knowing that time and experience are needed for development; perspective, having vision and ability to see down the road and suggest the next steps that a mentoree needs; and gifts and abilities that build up and encourage others.

MENTORING QUALITIES

In the book of Hebrews, we are encouraged to "remember your leaders, who spoke the word of God to you. Consider the outcome of their way of life and imitate their faith. Jesus Christ is the same yesterday and today and forever."[128]

A good mentor is honest with you, a model for you, deeply committed to you, open and transparent, a teacher, one who believes in your potential, one who can help you plan and turn your dream into reality, successful in your eyes, open to learning from you as well as teaching you, and willing to stay primarily on your agenda, not their own. More simply, a good mentor offers availability, confidentiality, honesty, accountability, boundaries, and evaluation.

A good mentoree is easy to believe in, easy to like and spend time with naturally, easy to keep helping, is like family, is teachable, one who respects his/her mentor, self-motivated, comfortable with and to

---

[128] Hebrews 13:7–8.

the mentor. More simply, a good mentoree contributes responsiveness, honesty, vulnerability, willingness to be accountable, commitment, and teachability.

To be an effective mentor and for the mentoring experience to be helpful, one or more of the following characteristics will be present:

- Intuition, ability to readily see potential in an individual
- Tolerance with mistakes, brashness, abrasiveness, and the like to see that potential develop
- Flexibility in responding to people and circumstances
- Patience, knowing that time and experience are needed for development
- Perspective, having vision and ability to see down the road and suggest the next steps that a mentoree needs
- Gifts and abilities that build up and encourage others

MENTORING CONTRACT

Establishing a mentoring contract is essential to effective mentoring and avoids the pitfalls experienced by many mentors and mentorees. The following guidelines were adapted from a trusted resource, *Connecting* by Stanley and Clinton.

THE TEN COMMANDMENTS OF MENTORING

1. Jointly agree on the purpose of the relationship. Present the objective(s) for the mentoring relationship. Determine the type of mentor needed. Identify the area(s) that need to be addressed.
2. Set the criteria for evaluation. What will a successful outcome look like? How will you know the objective(s) have been accomplished? Have the mentoree describe what he/she hopes to accomplish.
3. Determine the regularity of interaction. It should be a minimum of twice a month, but could be more, depending on the needs of

the mentoree and the availability of the mentor. It should begin as a three-month trial.

4. Determine accountability parameters—honesty, vulnerability, accountability, and whatever else is required by the mentor and agreed upon by the mentoree. What accountability parameters will be applied?

5. Set up communication mechanisms. Email, phone, face-to-face—whichever is the most convenient. At least one face-to-face meeting is required per month in addition to second or additional meetings by phone and/or email.

6. Clarify the level of confidentiality. What is shared on a personal level must remain confidential, unless it is of a legal nature (e.g., abuse of any kind, a crime, etc.)

7. Set the life cycle of the relationship. Three months for a preliminary timeframe, at the end of which each of you should evaluate the relationship. If you agree to continue, set an end date, not to exceed six additional months—a total of nine months.

8. Evaluate the relationship from time to time. Recommend an evaluation every two to three months.

9. Modify expectations to fit the real-life mentoring situation. If an issue or concern arises that needs more focused attention, the mentor and mentoree should decide whether the parameters of mentoring need to be changed.

10. Bring the mentoring relationship to a close. Celebrate the completion of the journey. Have the mentoree write about the experience and what was accomplished.

A guide by the side will help us reach our objectives, whether they be spiritual, emotional, intellectual, personal, or professional. We need mentors who will mentor us, peer mentors who will comentor us, and people we mentor. The result will be personal advancement toward realization of our potential, removal of destructive habits and sin, and provision of hope for a more productive and rewarding future.

QUESTIONS TO PONDER

What areas of your life need attention?

Who will you seek out to mentor you in these areas?

Who could benefit from your counsel and guidance?

RECOMMENDED RESOURCE

Connecting: The Mentoring Relationships You Need to Succeed (1992) by Paul Stanley and Robert Clinton

PLANNING (HOW TO DEVELOP A STRATEGIC PLAN)

In *Alice in Wonderland*, Alice says to the Cheshire Cat, "Would you tell me, please, which way I ought to go from here?"

"That depends a good deal on where you want to get to," said the Cat.

"I don't much care where," said Alice.

"Then it doesn't matter which way you go," said the Cat.

As with Alice, so with us. Without effective planning, we will have nowhere to go, and we'll just keep wandering aimlessly.

As a leader, sooner or later you will be faced with one or more of the following questions: Why is there so much confusion on what we are trying to accomplish? Why is there so much dissension and disagreement on our team? Why is there such a high turnover of people, especially in leadership positions? As a leader, why am I working twelve hours a day but can never keep up? Why have we failed on many projects? Why did God let us down? Why is the devil stopping us? The answer might be that your ministry lacks good long-term strategic thinking and planning!

Is planning unspiritual or unscriptural? Well, let's see what the Bible says about this concern. The Bible goes on to tell us that estimating the cost is smart;[129] everything should be done in a fitting and orderly way;[130] plans succeed when committed to the Lord;[131] whatever we do, we should do it as if we are working for the Lord;[132] godly counsel is a part of any successful plan;[133] and God is not a God of disorder.[134]

What do others say?

> Every enterprise requires commitment to common goals and shared values. Without such commitment there is no enterprise, there is only a mob.
>
> —Peter Drucker

> Many churches don't go out of existence, they go out of effectiveness.
>
> —Bill Hybels, Willow Creek

> Before you build a house, you need a blueprint. Before a plane leaves the tarmac, the pilot must file his flight plan with the tower. Before you do church as a team, there must be clear and concise understanding of the mission and assignment the Lord has given to that specific local church.

—Wayne Cordiero, New Hope Christian Fellowship

MINISTRY PLANNING PARADIGM

Before we develop a plan, we need to understand our primary overarching function, regardless of how we express it. For instance,

---

[129]   Luke 14:28.
[130]   1 Corinthians 14:40.
[131]   Proverbs 16:3.
[132]   Colossians 3:23.
[133]   Proverbs 15:22.
[134]   1 Corinthians 14:23.

"For the grace of God that brings salvation has appeared to all men. It teaches us to say 'No' to ungodliness and worldly passions, and to live self-controlled, upright and godly lives in this present age, while we wait for the blessed hope—the glorious appearing of our great God and Savior, Jesus Christ, who gave himself for us to redeem us from all wickedness and to purify for himself a people that are his very own, eager to do what is good."[135]

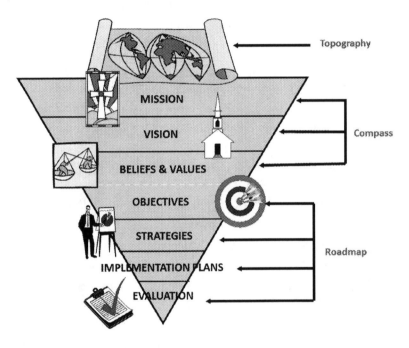

In a very general sense, ministry planning seeks certain answers. What are we trying to accomplish, generally? What does the target look like, specifically? What principles will we follow? What do we hope to accomplish? What strategies will help us get there? What processes will we use to get there? How do we plan to make progress? How can we stay on track?

In a graphical framework, ministry planning starts with broad

---

[135] Titus 2:11–14.

issues and becomes more specific the further you go down the inverted planning pyramid.

More specifically, effective ministry planning addresses seven key questions. The first three provide the compass of any ministry, and the last four provide the road map of any ministry.

How is an effective ministry plan developed and implemented? By prayerfully and carefully responding to the following seven questions:

1. What does the environment for ministry look like?

    • External and internal
    • Opportunities and needs
    • Trends and influences
    • Limitations and weaknesses

2. How would God want us to respond to the ministry environment?

    • Reliance upon God
    • General mission
    • Sphere of influence
    • Specific vision

3. What key principles will inform and guide our ministry activity?

    • Biblical assumptions (beliefs)
    • Core values

4. What are the major results we hope to obtain?

    • Quantifiable and nonquantifiable
    • Three-year objectives
    • Annual objectives

5. What strategies will we employ to reach our objectives?

- Winning
- Enfolding
- Equipping
- Deploying

6. How will the strategies be implemented?

  - Implementation plans
  - Quarterly SMART goals (specific, measurable, attainable, results oriented, time constrained)

7. How do we intend to evaluate our progress?

  - Performance standards
  - Monitoring (team meetings)
  - Control (team reports)
  - Feedback (remedial changes)

Ministry planning has one factor business strategic planning does not—the X factor and reliance upon God. The Lord foils the plans of the nations; he thwarts the purposes of the peoples. But the plans of the Lord stand firm forever, the purposes of his heart through all generations.[136]

Ministry plans that succeed rely on God himself to inform the process from beginning to end. If our ministry plans are to bring glory to God, five key inputs are essential: (1) guidance from the Bible, (2) intentional and persistent prayer, (3) empowerment from the Holy Spirit, (4) counsel from gifted and godly people, and (5) commitment to adjustment from above.

---

[136] Psalm 33:10–11.

MINISTRY PLANNING PROCESS

1. What does the environment for ministry look like? We need to join the tribe of Issachar, "who understood the times and knew what Israel should do."[137] This phase assesses where we are now and what we anticipate the ministry landscape will look like over the planning period. In this phase, we need to analyze the external (international, national, regional, and local) and internal (personnel, material, and financial resources) ministry environment. What trends/influences impact the ministry environment? What ministry opportunities present themselves? What needs are evident in these opportunities? What barriers or limitations exist in the ministry environment? What internal limitations and/or weaknesses must be overcome? What assumptions can we make about the future?

2. How would God want us to respond to the ministry environment? In this phase, we need to determine our mission and vision as they relate to the ministry environment, the sphere of influence God has called us to serve, and the needs we intend to meet, as seen from God's perspective in alignment with his purposes and according to his Word.

   Answer the following questions: Why do you exist? For what purpose? To meet what need? It provides the outermost boundary for your work. Correctly worded, it anchors you in the historic purposes of the church. It acts as a stabilizing influence by giving you a plumb line against which to evaluate opportunities and challenges. It expresses calling.

3. What key principles will inform and guide our ministry activity? What are our biblical beliefs about God, humankind, and ministry? What do we trust in, rely on, and cling to at our core? How do these central beliefs shape our personal attitudes and worldview? What are the key scriptural passages that will

---

[137] 1 Chronicles 12:32.

ensure we have God's perspective on who we are, why we exist, and what we will do? (No more than five to seven statements.)

Regarding values, what are the hills we are prepared to die on and the ministry principles we intend to live by? What are the guidelines we will adhere to? What rules will we follow?

4. What are the major results (objectives) we hope to obtain? Prescribe written, specific, and measurable objectives in the primary areas that contribute to the ministry's purpose. These are the key results desired upon completion of the planning; the targets you are shooting at—the bull's-eye representing exactly where you want to be at a certain point in time. This phase identifies where you want to be when all is said and done. These are the irreducible minimums you are shooting for and how you know you've arrived. They may include measurements, standards, benchmarks, yardsticks, or other criteria.

Objectives—and goals, for that matter—may include quantifiable or nonquantifiable objectives. Quantifiable objectives express numerical growth expectations, such as event attendance, new members, conversions, baptisms, small groups, new ministry programs, numbers of leaders trained and deployed, etc. Nonquantifiable objectives might include biblical literacy, skill development, vision ownership, etc.

5. What strategies will we employ to reach our objectives? Develop strategies on how to use available resources to meet objectives. Strategies are the links between objectives and results. These strategies are directly related to the mission, vision, beliefs, and values of the ministry organization.

In other words, if your mission is to win, enfold, equip, and deploy faithful followers of Jesus Christ, then each ministry area must have a strategy for each element of the mission statement.

This phase describes the major strategies we will employ to reach our stated objectives and provides the templates by which ministry is to be conducted. Key strategies might include processes, methods, systems, approaches, and techniques.

6. How will the strategies be implemented? Developing plans on how to staff, train, and evaluate personnel is critical to the success of the ministry plan. This is the "action" or "doing" step for all areas that are used to support the overall strategy.

This phase addresses organizational relationships, lines of authority, reporting relationships, and communication requirements necessary to effectively implement the strategic plan, in general, and the operational plans, specifically. This phase deals with the support mechanisms that need to be in place to provide adequate direction and resources for accomplishing the plans.

The following elements for each strategy: SMART goals, qualifying conditions, communications required, timelines (schedule), personnel needs, training plans, materials and resources, budget, and facility needs.

7. How do we intend to evaluate our progress? Set up control and evaluation procedures to determine if performance is keeping pace with attainment of objectives and if it is consistent with the defined purpose. The purposes of evaluation mechanisms are to accomplish ministry alignment, prioritize ministry accomplishment, encourage ministry assessment, coax ministry affirmation, embolden ministry correction, and elicit ministry improvement.

This phase depicts the mechanisms that will be used to report results, assess performance, and provide corrective feedback to the plan. Considerations may include determining what activities to measure and how to measure them, identification of reporting mechanisms, actual measurement of those activities, and comparing performance against the plan, evaluating results, and correcting measures, as needed.

An excellent resource to use in developing a strategic plan

for a church or a ministry plan for a specific ministry area is *Advanced Strategic Planning* by Aubrey Mulphurs.[138]

QUESTIONS TO PONDER

What ministry or organization where you are involved could benefit from strategic or ministry planning?

Who should participate in the planning?

In your current situation, how would you respond to the seven questions posed?

RECOMMENDED RESOURCE

Advanced Strategic Planning: A 21st Century Model for Church and Ministry Leaders, 3rd edition (2013) by Aubrey Malphurs

---

[138] Aubrey Mulphurs, *Advanced Strategic Planning: A 21st-Century Model for Church and Ministry Leaders,* 3rd edition (Grand Rapids: Baker Books, 2013).

REFRAMING (HOW TO USE FRAMING TO SOLVE PROBLEMS)

All leaders seek to make sense of the world around them through a set of perceptual attitudes more commonly referred to as a worldview. It is through that lens they view and interpret their surroundings, their relationships, and their perceptions of their observations. One could say they see the world through a frame.

While attending Harvard's Graduate School of Education, Institute for Educational Management, I was exposed to *Reframing Organizations* by Lee Bolman and Terrence Deal, now in its fifth edition.[139] This resource is an attempt to consolidate major schools of organizational thought into a comprehensive framework that encompasses four perspectives called frames. The authors suggest that, like maps, frames are both windows on a territory and tools for navigation.

There are four frames: structural, human resource, symbolic, and political. Each leader has a default frame through which he/she processes options, alternatives, possibilities, opportunities, choices, and prospects. What follows is a brief description of each frame, followed by applications derived by my use of the framing structure.

---

[139] Lee G. Bolman and Terrence E. Deal, *Reframing Organizations: Artistry, Choice, and Leadership*, 5th edition (San Francisco: Jossey-Bass/Wiley, 2013).

STRUCTURAL—FACTORY (ARCHITECTURE)

This frame is all about an organization as a factory. This frame depicts a rational world and emphasizes organizational architecture, including goals, structure, technology, specialized roles, coordination, and formal relationships. It is a rational model that simply looks at the facts to determine direction and action. Such organizations value org charts, allocate responsibilities, and create rules, policies, procedures, systems, and hierarchies to coordinate diverse activities into a unified effort. When something isn't working, some form of reorganization or redesign is needed to remedy the mismatch. General Electric and General Motors would be good examples of this frame.

HUMAN RESOURCE—FAMILIES (EMPOWERMENT)

This frame focuses on interpersonal relationships and sees an organization as an extended family, made up of individuals with needs, feelings, prejudices, skills, and limitations. The key challenge is to tailor the organization to individuals, finding ways for people to get the job done while feeling good about themselves and their work. Finding the right fit for people, this perspective contends, can only benefit the organization because members of the organization are operating from their sweet spot. Microsoft and Google would characterize this frame.

SYMBOLIC—TEMPLES (INSPIRATION)

This frame emphasizes ethos, culture, symbols, and spirit as keys to organizational success. The symbolic lens treats organizations as temples, tribes, or movements. These "cultures" are propelled by rituals, ceremonies, stories, heroes, and myths, rather than rules, policies, and managerial authority. These organizations are driven by well-established DNA consisting of mission, vision, and values. Departure from this DNA is tantamount to betrayal. Everything attempted or envisioned is seen through this DNA, with each actor on the stage playing his or her part. Starbucks and Apple would exemplify this frame.

POLITICAL—JUNGLES (ADVOCACY OR POLITICAL SAVVY)

This frame sees organizations as arenas, contests, or jungles. Parochial interests compete for power and scarce resources. Conflict is rampant because of enduring differences in needs, perspectives, and lifestyles among contending individuals and groups. Bargaining, negotiation, coercion, and compromise are a normal part of everyday life. Coalitions form around specific interests and change as issues come and go. Problems arise when power is concentrated in the wrong places or is so broadly dispersed that nothing gets done. Solutions arise from political skill and acumen. *The Apprentice* and *Survivor* reality TV series would correspond to this frame.

I believe reframing provides an excellent resource for leaders to process interpersonal engagements, analyze problems, evaluate conclusions, weigh alternative solutions, and consider competing options.

Reframing is helpful for the following situations: considering multiple options, reviewing several alternatives, processing a given approach to an initiative, preparing a presentation, developing a report or proposal, facilitating discussion, supervising the actions of subordinates, discerning the perspective of others, and seeing a given situation from a different viewpoint.

Effective leaders must resist the temptation to see any given issue, event, situation, or circumstance through their default frames until they have processed it through the other three frames first. Otherwise, they will simply reinforce a decision they have already made when examined through their preferred frame.

When people who reported to me sought approval for a conclusion they'd reached, I would ask them questions that focused on each of the four frames. I didn't reveal the strategy I was using. By asking them questions representing all four frames, I indirectly influenced them to consider the perspectives inherent with each frame. What might make sense in one frame might, in fact, make little sense when looked through the lens of the other frames. Or it might make more sense after processing it through all four frames.

When I did this with many employees, it became evident what I was doing. Many of them inquired where or why I did this, which provided a great opportunity to teach them the strategy to use with others who reported to them.

The significance of employing this strategy is that it will help leaders and teams to come to more viable positions and recommendations, as alternatives have been thoroughly processed through all four frames.

Let's look at four case studies to illustrate. The situations depicted focus on ministry settings, but with a little imagination they can be applied to any work setting. I believe the principles derived from each case study are applicable to all settings.

CASE STUDY 1

Imagine you are a young person, headed to the church office for your first day in a new job. You are inheriting a department with a reputation for slow, substandard service. Senior leadership credits much of the blame to your predecessor, who is viewed as too authoritarian and rigid. He is leaving the church for another position elsewhere, but he has agreed to stay on for a week to help you get oriented. One potential sticking point is that he hired most of your new staff. Many still feel loyal to him.

When you arrive, you get a frosty hello from the department administrative assistant. As you walk into your new office, you see the person you are replacing is behind the desk in a conversation with three other staff members. You say hello, and he responds, "Didn't the admin assistant tell you that we're in a meeting right now? If you'll wait outside, I'll be able to see you in about an hour."

What would you do? If you feel threatened or attacked—as most of us would—those feelings will push you toward either fight or flight. Fighting back and escalating the conflict is risky and could damage everyone. Backing away or fleeing could suggest that you are too emotional or not tough enough.

How would you respond, given the four frames?

Principle 1: Rather than flee or fight, go to the "balcony" to get a better perspective. Analyze the situation through each of the frames and select the appropriate frame for the situation, given the circumstances and people involved. Knowing the frame of the organization ahead of time will make the decision of how to respond easier.

CASE STUDY 2

Suppose a person who reports to you comes to you with a proposal. He has responsibility for small groups in the church but the requests to be in a small group have exceeded the number of groups currently in place. His proposal suggests that the solution is to recruit, train, and release additional leaders to lead more groups that will accommodate the increased requests. There is a limited pool of volunteers to draw from, and other departments must draw from the same pool. There is a budgetary impact.

Given the four frames, what questions would you ask him from each frame to help him process the proposal? What factors should he consider if he proceeds with the proposal? What issues and concerns might he consider if he implements the proposal? How would you help him think through the four frames?

Principle 2: When processing options, alternatives, choices, etc., set aside your default frame until you have processed the issue through the other three frames first. If you start with your default frame first, you simply will use the other frames to validate a decision you have already made.

CASE STUDY 3

You have developed a strategy to reach the community for Christ. The strategy will require engaging the community through acts of service to build trust and provide opportunities to share Christ. The strategy will require hiring a pastor of outreach not currently in the budget. You are requested to make a presentation to the congregation at large to justify the initiative and a new hire.

Knowing that formal and informal influencers representing all four of the frames will be at the meeting, many of whom are already contributing to the ministry with time, talent, and treasure, how would you craft your presentation?

Principle 3: Be prepared to address the unique characteristics associated with each frame in any scenario where many people are gathered. You can be sure there will be representatives for each frame in attendance. A good presentation anticipates this fact and prepares specifics of the presentation accordingly.

CASE STUDY 4

You have spent a great deal of time developing a ministry strategy that departs from anything you have done in the past. What you have been doing is no longer producing the results desired. You want to change your ministry philosophy and approach, which will require retooling your staff and volunteers. This will take time and money to accomplish. You believe the strategy will be a game-changer. You are committed to the strategy but need the approval of your supervisor, whose default frame is different from your own. Your supervisor's default frame is [blank].

How would you craft your argument to get a hearing and possibly secure the approval of your supervisor?

Principle 4: Normally we prepare our arguments based on our default frame. If you want to be heard and possibly secure a positive response to your request, you should learn the default frame of the person whose approval you seek. This is not manipulation but a sign of respect that you have thought through the issues and concerns of the person from whom you want approval.

I can assure you that this is a wonderful tool to use to effectuate an applicable response to a host of issues. I have used the strategy with compelling results. Hopefully, this will help you become a good leader, known for arriving at great solutions for complex problems or securing difficult approval for worthwhile initiatives.

QUESTIONS TO PONDER

What is your default frame?

What are the default frames of people to whom you report?

How would you have handled a situation you encountered in the past, had you known the frames of others involved?

RECOMMENDED RESOURCE

Reframing Organizations: Artistry, Choice, and Leadership, 6th edition (2017) by Lee G. Bolman and Terrence E. Deal

PROJECTING (HOW TO ESTABLISH GOALS TO REACH DESIRED OBJECTIVES)

The only time you are guaranteed a 100 percent success rate is when you aim at nothing; you are destined to reach it—nothing. Effective and efficient planning and implementation of key objectives—be they annual, trimester, or quarterly—will help ensure that leaders make meaningful progress and reach their outcomes.

In strategic or tactical planning, we brainstorm a preferable future by seriously considering the implications of the following questions:

- What are we doing now that we need to *keep* doing but do better?
- What are we doing now that we need to *change* doing if we are to succeed?
- What are we doing now that we need to *stop* doing?
- What are we *not* doing now that we need to *start* doing?

Answering these thought-provoking questions will help leaders and their teams look at new possibilities, options, and alternative solutions to a specific problem, a new initiative, or a prescribed objective.

Generally, once an environmental analysis (external and internal) is completed in a strategic planning exercise, vision is formed about a new or better future as an organization. This vision is informed, conditioned, and established by agreed-upon assumptions, beliefs, and operating values. Objectives are formulated, and applicable strategies are identified to reach those objectives. Each objective might include one or more strategies for reaching an objective.

It's the proverbial "rubber meets the road" in the implementation. This is the action or doing step for all areas that are used to support the overall strategy. This phase addresses organizational relationships, lines of authority, reporting relationship, and communication requirements necessary to effectively implement the strategic plan, in general, and the operational plans, specifically. This phase deals with the support mechanisms that need to be in place to provide adequate direction and resources for accomplishing the plans.

An implementation plan may include the following elements for each strategy: SMART goals, qualifying conditions, communications required, timelines (schedule), personnel needs, training plans, materials and resources, budget, and facility needs.

One of the most effective management tools used to plan and implement key objectives and strategies is the use of SMART goals, the focus of our discussion today.

SETTING GOALS

Establishing performance goals helps a leader, manager, supervisor, or project team move in a straight line toward accomplishing long-term objectives via key strategies. Team members need to have a part in determining the goals, but in the final analysis, they are the leader's goals.

From a scriptural perspective, then, planning using SMART goals redeems the time[140] and helps us to be stewards of God's precious resources and to focus our efforts, according to his plan.[141]

Regardless of your context, one of the most effective management

---

[140] Ephesians 5:15c16; Colossians 4:50.
[141] Psalm 20:4; 33:11; Isaiah 32:8; Jeremiah 29:11.

tools used to plan and implement key objectives and strategies is the use and application of SMART goals. Goals are simply a means to that end. Goals are the steps, tactics, programs, recipes, tasks, courses, or operations we intend to use to make and mark progress.

SMART GOAL GUIDELINES

They are *s*pecific, *m*easurable, *a*ttainable, *r*esults oriented, and *t*ime constrained. Thus, they are called *SMART* goals. Before examples of SMART goals are presented, let's look more closely at what makes a good goal.

Is the goal specific? Most goals fail initially because they are not specific enough. Is the goal clear enough that a team can see it? Or is it so open-ended that you'll never know if you attained it at all? Is the goal specific enough?

Is the goal measurable? Measurement can be either quantitative or qualitative. Quantitative goals can be numerical or based on percentage of completion. Qualitative goals may include the presence of observable but nonquantifiable traits. Is the goal quantifiably or qualitatively measurable?

Is the goal attainable? Overzealous, unrealistic goals outlined may not be attainable. The onus for attainability rests with those who are tasked with attaining the goal. Attainability is based on the expertise, experience, talent, competence of the team, and resources available to the team. Is the goal attainable in terms of the capabilities and capacity of the team?

Is the goal results oriented? What is the purpose of the goal? What is the stated end that is to be attained? How will you know if the goal is reached and that it indeed contributes to the objective sought? What is the aim of the goal? Is the goal results oriented in that it adequately points to a recognizable outcome? In other words, what is its stated purpose?

Is the goal time constrained? What is the time frame selected to attain the goal? My experience suggests that a goal should not be any longer than four months. Three-month (quarterly) goals are preferred. If a goal is longer than that time frame, it should be divided into smaller time increments. Is the goal time constrained, in that it progressively leads to the desired outcome whether it is laid out in time increments or progressive steps?

Each strategy should have SMART goals associated with its implementation.

Objectives can be annual and represent key results expected. To reach the objective, one or more strategies (processes, methods, systems, techniques, procedures, etc.) may be implemented. Each strategy may have one or more SMART goals associated with it.

For instance, to reach an objective, three strategies will be implemented. Each strategy will include two or more SMART goals, designed to employ the strategy.

Although SMART goals can be written to encompass any time frame, they usually cover three to four months. These goals also may be written in terms of steps necessary to fully implement the strategy.

SMART goals can be represented by a time frame (e.g., week, month, quarter, trimester) or a succession of events built on one another, leading to completion of the strategy. Most SMART goals use a designated time frame, even if it takes three or more goals to complete the task. The task is broken up into defined increments of time.

Regarding a succession of events, SMART goals may be written as follows. Let's assume you were given the strategy to provide qualified individual contributors to a program manager, who is responsible for the design and manufacture of a system. One SMART goal might be to evaluate your personnel resources. A follow-on goal might be to provide training in the competencies needed by the program. A third goal might be to implement a probationary period, concluding with an evaluation of the employee's effectiveness by the program manager.

As a leader, manager, or supervisor, your job is to maintain the integrity of the SMART goal framework, not necessarily the specifics on how the details of the goal are determined—that should be the responsibility of the project team members, if possible.

More simply stated, as leader, manager, or supervisor, your

responsibility is primarily to ensure that the employee adheres to the framework of the SMART goal.

EXAMPLES

The examples that follow address a ministry context. I hope you will readily see how they can be adjusted for a nonministry context, if that is your operational setting.

- Form a ministry team (specific) to help children process the trauma of their parents' divorce (results oriented) by the end of February [year] (time constrained), as evidenced by the selection of curriculum and the scheduling of course dates (measurable/nonquantifiable).
- Increase the number of small groups (specific) by 25 percent (measurable/quantifiable), beginning in March [year] (time constrained), for reaching those members and regular attenders who have not been involved in small groups and who need intimate fellowship and care (results oriented).
- Form a mentoring ministry for women (specific) to assist them in becoming followers of Jesus Christ by establishing a relationship with another woman, who will help them grow spiritually (results oriented), as evidenced by their commitment to Bible study, prayer, fellowship, and witnessing (measurable/nonquantifiable). Training will be conducted in January [year] for mentors, and the program launched in March [year] (time constrained).

SMART goals contain action verbs, such as assess, plan, design, develop, recruit, fund, train, schedule, promote, establish, produce, communicate, conduct, review, evaluate, assess, assign, critique, select, etc.

SMART goals can be developed for personal as well as professional purposes. Wherever I have led others, I have used SMART goals with success. I hope this information will help you become a more effective and efficient leader, manager, or supervisor.

QUESTIONS TO PONDER

Are your objectives and goals specific and measurable, attainable (realistic), results oriented, and time constrained?

What are your personal objectives and goals? Are they SMART?

What are your professional objectives and goals? Are they SMART?

RECOMMENDED RESOURCE

Project Management for the Unofficial Project Manager (2015) by Kory Kogon, Suzette Blakemore, and James Wood

COMMUNICATING (HOW TO COMMUNICATE EFFECTIVELY)

All good relationships, at the root, have a genuine concern for the well-being and welfare of others within the relationship. The Bible calls this love. It is action oriented. Love is patient and kind; it does not envy; it is not proud or rude or self-seeking or easily angered. It keeps no record of wrongs, does not delight in evil, and rejoices with the truth. Love always protects, always trusts, always hopes, and always perseveres.[142]

"A new command I give you: Love one another. As I have loved you, so you must love one another. By this all men will know that you are my disciples, if you love one another." "Let no debt remain outstanding, except the continuing debt to love one another, for he who loves his fellowman has fulfilled the law. Dear friends, let us love one another, for love comes from God. Everyone who loves has been born of God and knows God."[143]

MAINTAINING GOOD RELATIONSHIPS

Mac Hammond of Hammond Ministries helps us understand the importance of relationships. He believes an effective leader with poor

---

[142] 1 Corinthians 13:1–7.

[143] John 13:34–35; Romans 13:8; 1 John 4:7.

relational skills is almost a contradiction in terms. Ninety-nine percent of all the good things you'll ever receive in life are going to come through the channel of relationships. Nearly every form of blessing and increase comes as a direct result of relationships with other people. When God wants to get something to you, he does it through the vehicle of relationships. When he wants to encourage you, you don't hear a booming voice from heaven saying, "Be thou encouraged." No, he sends someone to you to put an arm around you and say a few words that turn your day around. That's why the quality of your relationships and your skill in cultivating them has a profound impact on your effectiveness as a leader.

Positive relationships are important. Maintaining fellowship and good relationships is a major key to accomplishing tasks in a ministry team. Broken fellowship destroys trust and alienates the members. All relationships evolve around personal needs; they are altered by contact and are constantly changing. Needs that are met will build relationships; unmet needs will erode relationships.

FOUR RELATIONSHIP STYLES

There are four basic relationship styles: cooperation, retaliation, domination, and isolation. All relationships begin in a cooperation style and remain there if all needs within the relationship are met. An unmet need causes the person with the need to move to a retaliation style to get his or her need met. Eventually, a winner and loser appear. The domination style now begins. The winner dominates the person losing the struggle. After time, the person being dominated concludes he/she is being rejected. That person may take the next step to an isolation style. This is the last phase of the deteriorating relationship before it is terminated.

The further one moves away from the cooperation style, the lower productivity drops in the ministry team. The greatest level of team spirit and satisfaction is maintained within the cooperation style. If the cooperation style is not maintained, then a gradual disintegration of the relationship ensues. Team leaders should be aware of the characteristics of this disintegration. By observing the behaviors of their team members, they may be able to stop the disintegration before it is too late.

Cooperation style: There will be a commitment to meet the other's needs. Mutual trust and respect will exist. There will be mutual utilization of personal gifts, skills, and creativity. Problems will be solved jointly. Productivity will increase. Commitment to the relationship will grow.

Retaliation style: There will be attempts to make the other person conform to what you want done. Aggressive action toward the other person is eventually taken. The other person becomes an object in the way, not a person with his or her own needs. A struggle for domination begins. There is a period of perpetual conflict. Eventually, there appears to be a winner and a loser.

Domination style: The "winner" controls the "loser." The loser's personality is suffocated. Each loses respect for the other. The loser's creativity is lost. The loser resorts to manipulation. The loser gives up, concluding that the situation is hopeless, and the relationship will not improve.

Isolation style: The other person is mentally blocked out. Communication stops. Both develop mistrust of the other. Problems remain unresolved. Needs remain unmet. Each develops unconcern for the other's needs. Productivity within the relationship drops drastically. The relationship terminates.

RESTORING COOPERATIVE RELATIONSHIPS

The following steps are recommended for restoring cooperative relationships. The team leader may facilitate this process. If the deteriorating situation is between the team leader and another member of the team, then the team leader should personally follow the same process. On occasion, it may be necessary to take the entire team through the process.

- Recognize the need for the relationship.
- Admit the style you are currently in.
- Admit your contribution to the problem.

- Ask for forgiveness.
- Make the conscious decision to restore the relationship to cooperation.
- Begin to put the needs of the other person ahead of yours.
- Show appreciation for the other person's contribution to restoring the relationship.

RULES FOR RIGHT RELATIONSHIPS

The following rules of engagement are suggested in any interaction between the team leader and team members or between team members. These working principles apply in any interactive situation. Attack the problem, not the person. Verbalize feelings, but don't act them out. Forgive in place of judging. Give more than you take.

TEN WAYS TO IMPROVE RELATIONAL SKILLS

In an article posted on the internet by Richard Krejcir (1980),[144] "10 Ways to Improve Relational Skills" were presented.

1. Speak to people. There is nothing as nice as a cheerful word of greeting.
2. Smile at people. It takes seventy-two muscles to frown, only fourteen to smile.
3. Call people by name. The sweetest music to anyone's ear is the sound of one's own name.
4. Be friendly and helpful. If you would like to have friends, then be friendly.
5. Be cordial. Speak and act as if everything you do were a genuine pleasure. If it is right and good, it really should be.
6. Be genuinely interested in people. Empathy means involvement.
7. Be generous with praise and cautious with criticism.
8. Be considerate with the feelings of others. It will be appreciated.

---

[144] Richard J. Krejcir, "10 Ways to Improve Relational Skills," *Into Thy Word* (1980), www.intothyword.org/apps/articles/default.asp?articleid'32152.

9. Be thoughtful of the opinions of others. There are three sides to controversy—yours, the others, and the right one.

10. Be alerted to give service. What counts most in life is who we are in Christ and then what we do for others.

DEVELOPING COMMUNICATION SKILLS

Communication Fidelity

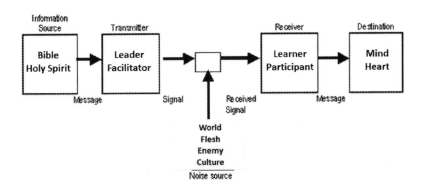

Communication can be defined as the process we go through to convey understanding from one person or group to another. Communication involves a message that represents the intention of the sender, the sender of the message, the medium through which the message is sent, a receiver of the message, and inherent barriers associated with each of the elements of communication (e.g., message, sender, medium, and receiver).

Barriers are a part of a communication process and may hinder the communication process. Such barriers may include ambient noise around the sender or the receiver; temperature of the room; faulty acoustics or other physical distractions; the speaker's communication style, such as rate of speech and vocal variety (inflection); mannerisms or appearance of the speaker; interruptions, such as phone calls, outside noises, etc.; time pressures or deadlines; the time of day; cultural issues, such as ethnicity, geography, age, gender, religion, values, etc.; language; past experiences; perceptions and biases; and mental filters, such as opinions, attitudes or worldview, beliefs, values, motives, emotions, and knowledge.

The goal in effective communication is to make sure the idea and feeling sent is the idea and feeling received. Poor communications between team members can erode positive relationships within the team.

THE ROLE OF NONVERBAL COMMUNICATION

Studies have shown that most ideas and feelings are transmitted nonverbally. What you *do* communicates far more than what you *say*. Fifty-five percent of the message is communicated nonverbally. Thirty-eight percent is communicated through the tone of voice; that is, how it is said. Seven percent is communicated by actual words; that is, what you say.[145]

Nonverbal forms of communication—93 percent of all communication—may include body language, facial expressions, gestures, touch, proxemics (personal space distances), dress or appearance, posture, eye contact, and demeanor. Many of these forms are not conscious activities. They may simply reflect habitual actions developed over a lifetime, yet they can distract the listener from hearing what is said.

THE IMPORTANCE OF ACTIVE LISTENING

Since approximately 90 percent of the message is communicated nonverbally, the listener must make sure the message is translated properly. Active listening focuses on the actions and tone of voice, as

---

[145] These statistics come from "Communication without Words," published in *Psychology Today* in 1968, based on research done by Albert Mehrabain.

well as the words being spoken. Active listening includes the following techniques:

- Reflecting the feelings of the speaker
- Being aware of verbal and nonverbal cues
- Having an attitude of acceptance
- Recognize individual differences (gender, culture, temperament, etc.)
- Displaying the respect and understanding of the speaker's ability, values, and ideas
- Letting the other person explore alternatives
- Asking clarifying questions
- Paraphrasing and checking for understanding
- Summarizing for clarity and understanding
- Expressing empathy, hearing yourself—tone and words
- Having a sincere interest in what the person says
- Allowing enough time for the person to express himself/herself
- Allowing the person to express his/her thoughts, feelings, and opinions without judgment
- Using good eye contact, avoiding negative gestures, watching body language
- Giving positive feedback and recognition when possible

The US Navy trains instructors to pay attention to VEGA, an acronym for voice, eyes, gestures, and attitude. Instructors should use voice inflection and avoid monotones. They should also look around the audience regularly, avoiding focusing on one or a few persons. They should avoid annoying gestures, like looking away from the person communicating with them, playing with change in their pockets, and making overt gestures with the hands. Finally, they should convey a positive attitude during the conversation, expressing an interest in what is being said. These principles can be applied in active listening.

THREE POOR LISTENING HABITS TO AVOID

- Mentally jumping to a conclusion before the team member has finished speaking.
- Formulating a response and not paying close attention while the team member is speaking.
- Focusing on how the person communicates rather than on what is being communicated.

More simply, practice the following, and you will develop good active-listening skills: be attentive, remain silent, avoid distractions, focus on the message, express interest, use positive nonverbal signals, don't interrupt, restate and paraphrase, ask questions, ask for examples, and summarize.

HELPFUL COMMUNICATION HINTS

In selecting the content of a message and the arrangement and ordering of the content, the sender should take into consideration the receiver's communication skills, attitudes, knowledge level, social position, and culture.

The sender should use more than one communication channel to achieve maximum effectiveness. Sensory channels include sight, sound, touch, smell, and taste. Institutionalized channels include face-to-face conversation, printed materials, and electronic media.

The sender should strive to ensure accurate message relay by insisting on adequate feedback. Adequate feedback may consist of rephrasing what was received, repeating back what was heard, or restating what was understood. Such feedback reduces miscommunication, determines proximity of meanings, and measures comprehension and acceptance.

All of us, whether a leader or a follower, need to learn how to communicate effectively. Just knowing the elements of communication fidelity shows us how a message can lose its clarity by the time it gets to the receiver. Watching someone's nonverbals can often tell us more about what is really being communicated than the spoken word.

When I was pastoring in a church in San Diego, I interviewed thirty-three men to determine who would be invited to participate in a ministry designed to help them grow spiritually. As I interviewed them, I watched their nonverbals more than I listened to their words. I selected thirteen men, based primarily on their body language when I interviewed them. If they leaned forward in the conversation, looked me in the eye, expressed an excited demeanor, and demonstrated some degree of passion for what was being offered, they were in. Otherwise, they were not in the initial group.

QUESTIONS TO PONDER

What listening techniques do you need to cultivate?
When you communicate with others, what nonverbals are presented?
How can you improve your communication skill?

RECOMMENDED RESOURCE

Communication Skills: A Practical Guide to Improving Your Social Intelligence, Presentation, Persuasion and Public Speaking (2015) by Ian Tuhovsky and Wendell Wadsworth

SOLVING (HOW TO SOLVE PROBLEMS EFFECTIVELY AND EFFICIENTLY)

It is pleasant to see plans develop. That is why fools refuse
to give them up even when they are wrong.[146]

Problem solving requires prayer, patience, nurturing, good communication, and teamwork. It also takes a willingness to push ourselves beyond the usual methods for looking for solutions. The church and ministry organizations are faced with problems every day. Good decisions must be made, especially in the face of growing economic constraints and limited resources. Many of us have solved problems, only to find out that we answered the wrong questions. In other words, we either addressed the symptoms and not the cause, or we provided a solution for the wrong problem. There is no fail-proof method for solving problems. There are fundamental procedures that, when applied to a given problem, will produce more effective solutions.

---

[146] Proverbs 13:19.

PREPARATION FOR PROBLEM SOLVING

Pray and ask for godly wisdom. Prayer is the oil that lubricates the mind and heart for processing factors that influence and impact the problem being addressed and for arriving at God-honoring solutions.

Make the time you need for uninterrupted thought. Since new ideas don't always arrive on schedule, this must be done almost daily. Take a walk, go to a study place, go for a drive, or find a place where you won't be interrupted.

Read about the problem you have identified. Reading is a proven way to stimulate your mind so that you come up with novel ideas. Search the scriptures for similar situations. Take advantage of libraries at the church, the seminary, city, colleges, universities, or the internet.

Capture your thoughts as they occur. This is helpful not only because you may forget some of the best ideas but also because not all of them will be immediately useful. Build a file and look at it often.

Get input from others. Use your committee members, associates, team members, and friends as sounding boards. Get their thinking on the issue. Any ideas you bring away could be useful, even if they are not as interested as you are in the problem.

STEPS IN PROBLEM SOLVING

The following method for solving problems has been used extensively in both private industry and government agencies. It is designed to guide the leader through a specific process in arriving at an effective solution. The effectiveness of this simple process rests on the giftedness, discipline, diligence, thoroughness, and objectivity of the problem solvers.

1. Clearly state the problem.
2. Identify the cause of the problem.
3. Identify the change needed.
4. Determine what is to be gained or lost.
5. Identify the alternatives.
6. State the cost of each alternative.
7. Choose between the alternatives.

8. Delegate action steps.

9. Evaluate progress and results.

A more detailed approach may be needed to ensure the accuracy, relevance, and applicability of a solution to a particularly thorny or complex problem. In this case, the problem solvers should address each of the steps suggested and consider every question asked. Not all the questions or considerations may apply in each situation. Nevertheless, they should be reviewed.

Although out of print, *Management for Your Church* (1984), by Alvin J. Lindgren and Norman Shawchuck, presented a model for problem analysis that remains as one of the best approaches to solving problems. According to these experts, four components comprise a problem-solving system: (1) problem analysis: identifying and defining the problem and its cause; (2) decision analysis: planning the course of action most likely to solve the problem; (3) implementation: carrying out the action plan; and (4) evaluation: measuring the extent to which the plan is working and modifying it accordingly.[147]

The process includes the following steps:

PROBLEM ANALYSIS

According to Lindgren and Shawchuck, church committees usually approach problem-solving efforts by dealing with problems, causes, and solutions without distinguishing which is which. As they continue the discussion, they jump from one subject to another, and as each new subject is introduced, the attention of the group is turned toward it for a while, only soon to veer away to another newly introduced subject. Members of the group seldom agree on what the real problem is because they mean different things when they refer to a problem. Therefore, some are discussing problems, some are discussing causes, and others are discussing solutions—all being set forth as the problem.

---

[147] Norman Shawchuck and Alvin J. Lindgren, *Management for Your Church: How to Realize Your Church's Potential through a Systems Approach* (Organizational Resources Press, 1984), 32–44.

A problem, the authors contend, is an unwanted effect or an unsatisfied need. As such, a problem is always a deviation from a desired performance (objective) or result. A cause of a problem is always an unwanted change in some distinctive feature of the system that causes the deviation. This may be a single event or condition or a combination of events or conditions operating as one. A decision is a choice of action to solve a problem, a hoped-for solution.

The authors go on to state, "Every problem has only one real cause, which is either one single event or condition or several that have combined to act as if there were but one single cause. So, a search for cause is always a search for one specific change or a combination of changes that have produced the unwanted effect. Secondly, a problem cannot be solved unless its cause is known. Attempting to solve a problem without knowing its cause is the fundamental reason for failures in problem-solving efforts. Finally, a problem is solved by dealing with the event or condition causing it. Emergency, stopgap action may be taken to forestall the consequences of the problem, but the problem will remain until its cause has been discovered and dealt with."[148]

PROBLEM AWARENESS

State the problem as clearly as possible. The deviation from some objective or desired result is the problem. Something has happened to upset the status quo. A situation, event, or result has created ministry disequilibrium. What is the desired objective, and how has the current situation deviated from the desired objective?

PROBLEM PRIORITY

Determine the priority of the problem. Three considerations are important: time, effect, and trend. Are there any time pressures to solve it? What will be the effects if it is not solved? Is the situation getting better or worse? Is there a reasonable hope for solving it? Is there a way of knowing when the problem is solved?

---

[148] Ibid., 104.

PROBLEM DIMENSIONS

Determine the dimensions of the problem. This step specifies precisely what the problem is or is not and draws a boundary that clearly separates the problem from every other activity, issue, or group in the church or ministry organization.

Identifying problem dimensions answers the questions of what, where, when, how bad, and how many. What specific group or groups are involved? Where, specifically, is the problem located? Precisely, when did the problem first occur? Exactly how many people are involved in the problem? How often does the problem occur?

CHARACTERISTICS AND DISTINCTIONS

Determine the distinctions between the *is* and the *is not* characteristics of the problem. What is distinctive about these characteristics? What makes the group involved different from other groups? What is distinctive about the where, when, and what of the characteristics?

In "How to Solve It,"[149] George Polya, a mathematician, makes the following suggestions regarding determining characteristics and distinctions of a problem. Discuss it. Ask questions about it. Draw a picture of it. Restate it in your own words. Tell someone else about it. Restate the information given. Restate the question. Can you find a pattern in the data?

CHANGES IN DISTINCTIONS

Identify the changes that have occurred to produce the distinctions or within any area of distinction. This step is aimed at finding possible causes by identifying changes in the distinctive areas that possibly could have caused the deviation. This requires carefully sifting through the distinctions, identifying all the changes that have taken place to cause the distinctions, or that have taken place within the distinctions.

---

[149] George Polya, "How to Solve It: A New Aspect of Mathematical Method," https://notendur.hi.is/hei2/teaching/Polya_HowToSolveIt.pdf.

CAUSE FORMULATION

Determine which change is the most likely cause of the problem and how this may be tested for validity. This step involves three stages: (1) identifying all the changes that might possibly have caused the problem, (2) determining the one change that is most likely to be the cause, and (3) testing the most likely cause to see whether it did in fact cause the problem.

DECISION ANALYSIS AND IMPLEMENTATION

This step determines the course of action that will most likely solve the problem.

PROBLEM AND CAUSE FORMULATION

How well can we describe the problem to be solved? What is the most likely cause of this problem? What are the theological, missional, organizational, and interpersonal aspects of this problem? In which system component does the problem lie (e.g., input, transforming, output, boundaries, feedback loop, environment)?

Input system: Those elements needed to carry out a function, process, procedure, methodology, or strategy. It might include purposes such as mission, vision, beliefs or values, an objective, a recruitment process, the audience to which the effort is focused, a ministry plan, or some other element that sets the framework for the transforming system.

For example, the church might have an objective of assimilating regular attenders into a caring small group. This would require an implementation plan requiring recruitment of leaders, training, promotion of the groups, etc.

Transforming system: This element might include a ministry program, function, process, procedure, methodology, or strategy designed to meet agreed-upon objectives associated with the mission, vision, values, and beliefs of the church or ministry organization. When something is broken, we tend to focus on the transforming system alone. We either revise it or replace it with something else. The problem may not be with the transforming system; it may be with one of the other systems (e.g., input, output, boundaries, feedback loop, etc.).

For example, the transforming system for small groups might include an organizational structure for small groups, a format for small-group meetings, a training program for leaders, development of materials, formation of groups, scheduling, and conduct of small-group meetings, etc.

Output system: This element addresses the results one hopes to attain by the transforming system. This system exports the ministry program, function, process, procedure, methodology, or strategy to various constituencies (e.g., church members, visitors, the community, etc.) in accordance with expected results.

For example, the output system in our illustration might include the small groups themselves, the recognition program for small-group leaders, the expansion of the small-group ministry, and evaluation process for determining the effectiveness of the small-group ministry, etc.

System Evaluation

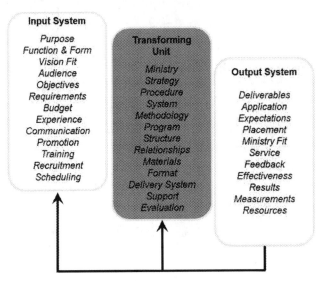

What is broken?

When an implemented program fails to produce the outcomes we expected or anticipated, we tend to jettison it for something new. We may not realize that the program itself may not be broken; it may be because the input or output system has failed us. We may have failed to properly introduce the new program. The input system is broken. Or we have misjudged who will benefit from such a program, how it should be applied, what service it is designed to serve, or the results we can expect.

Boundaries: This element might include the approval process, corporate mission, vision, values, budgetary constraints, physical facilities, availability of supervisory personnel, availability of leadership, appropriate materials and resources, church or ministry organizational traditions, historical precedents, constituency concerns, conflicting priorities, another system's interference, etc.

Feedback loop: This element could include such things as staff morale, congregational response, evaluation results, leadership turnover, lack of participation or commitment, preventive and corrective measures, changing financial support, redistribution of personnel and material resources, etc.

Environment: This element could include external and internal environmental issues such as governmental regulations, changing needs, regional concerns, denominational influences, cultural issues, demographic shifts, neighborhood issues, pastoral staff changes, changes in organizational purposes, etc.

Objectives: What do we want to accomplish in solving this problem? What are the specific issues that need to be confronted in meeting these objectives? If these issues are resolved, will we know the problem has been solved?

Resources and constraints: What conditions in the church or ministry organization and the environment (external and internal) will help or hinder this course of action? Can the constraints be reduced? How? What time, facilities, and people are available for achieving the objectives? Have you ever previously solved a problem like this?

Criteria: How will we know when the problem has been solved? What will be different? How will we measure the degree to which our objectives have been met and the problem has been solved? What are the requirements of a good set of conditions to solve this problem? When will each of these decisions be needed, and by whom?

Decision: What course of action will most likely solve the problem? What will the results of this decision look like? How will we evaluate our problem-solving effort?

Several steps are suggested for identifying more creative ideas.

Generate ideas: That's all you want to do at this stage—no evaluations, just inspiration. Put all the ideas on paper, a whiteboard, or cards. Later, you can organize, relate, combine, or eliminate these ideas.

Evaluate strengths: Now ask, "What's good about this idea?" If you can't come up with anything to recommend it, go to the next idea on the list. Do not touch on the negatives or weaknesses at this point. If a part of a group, keep the discussion focused only on the positive. Ideas drawing early criticism tend to meet a premature death.

Evaluate weaknesses: Start looking for drawbacks. Then compare the strengths and weaknesses. Those ideas with overwhelming negative points and weak positive ones can be eliminated.

Process through frames: See the chapter on Reframing in this book. The key is to process and evaluate the ideas through each of the frames—structural, human resource, political, and symbolic. Make sure you save your default frame—the one you naturally use in concluding the viability of possible alternatives—for last.

Choose the best solution: You are now ready to choose from the best of the lot. Because every idea was treated with respect while it was being generated and evaluated, the final selection is likely to be constructive and productive. If this course of action for solving the problem should prove unsatisfactory, what are the alternatives?

Implementation: Who is the person or the group who needs to approve this plan before it can become functional? How should the plan be implemented? Why is it necessary? Where should it be done? When should it be done? Who should do it? What should be done? How should it be done?

CREATIVE PROBLEM-SOLVING TECHNIQUES

The following problem-solving techniques will produce creative solutions to problems.

1. Brainstorming

This method is used to draw ideas out of a group. Evaluation will take place later. Everyone tosses in any idea related to the subject, no matter how far out it may seem. A recorder writes down ideas submitted by members of the group. No one may ask questions except for clarification. No critical discussion is permitted at this point. Building on the ideas of others should be encouraged.

2. Five sensing

Once the ideas have been given, the next step is to "five-sense" them. This process is used to expand a thought or idea. Five sensing is thinking consciously with all known senses—sight, sound, taste, touch, and smell. It involves more detailed brainstorming by focusing on how the five senses affect or contribute to the concept or thought.

3. Idea countering

Once the brainstorming is completed the next step is to counter the ideas. This method weeds out or justifies an idea of questionable value. The group examines each questionable idea, and a decision is made to keep the idea or throw it out.

4. Storyboarding

Walt Disney invented this visual planning technique. It involves the use of walls, cards, markers, and pins. Each idea is placed on a small card and posted on the wall or storyboard. As the planning session is conducted, the ideas (cards) can be moved or discarded as needed. The storyboard helps keep ideas and thoughts organized and visible during the entire planning session.

Other creative problem-solving techniques are readily available online. The following websites offer a multitude of techniques for creative problem solving. Check them out.

- Project Renaissance CPS Techniques[150]
- Creative Thinking Methods and Techniques[151]

---

[150] Win Wenger, "CPS Techniques," *Project Renaissance*, http://www.winwenger. com/mind.htm.

[151] Chris Dickman, "Creative Thinking Methods and Techniques," *StockLogos*, December 29, 2014, http://members.ozemail.com.au/~caveman/Creative/ Techniques/

QUESTIONS TO PONDER

How do you solve problems in your organization?

How can you apply these ideas in your work setting?

What would you add, change, or delete in solving problems?

RECOMMENDED RESOURCE

The COACH Model for Christian Leaders: Powerful Leadership Skills for Solving Problems, Reaching Goals, and Developing Others (2012) by Keith E. Webb and Gary R. Collins

RESOLVING (HOW TO RESOLVE PERSONAL CONFLICTS)

In what settings does conflict arise? What kinds of conflicts have you experienced over the last six months? What kinds of conflicts may arise in a ministry setting or organizational setting? What conflict management styles have you seen employed? How do you resolve conflicts? What process do you use?

When two or more people engage in activity where personal interests, boundaries, beliefs, and value come into play, conflict is inevitable. Well-meaning people involved in worthwhile projects come into conflict all the time. Since conflict is unavoidable, how we manage such conflict becomes crucial. Conflict is not necessarily bad. New insights, perspectives, and options are often forged over the anvil of conflict. How we manage relationships amid conflict can be life-giving or life-draining, depending on motives and approaches used in resolving such conflicts.

Since our focus is the development of lay leaders, conflict generally arises among members of a team. Someone's feelings get hurt or are disregarded; someone tries an end-around with another team member; someone tries to control the process toward a specific outcome; someone doesn't like the approach to a particular issue and creates a barrier to completion—and on and on it goes.

Of course, we have a scriptural model for resolving personal conflicts.

> If your brother sins against you, go and show him his fault, just between the two of you. If he listens to you, you have won your brother over. But if he will not listen, take one or two others along, so that 'every matter may be established by the testimony of two or three witnesses.' If he refuses to listen to them, tell it to the church; and if he refuses to listen even to the church, treat him as you would a pagan or a tax collector. "I tell you the truth, whatever you bind on earth will be bound in heaven, and whatever you loose on earth will be loosed in heaven." Again, I tell you that if two of you on earth agree about anything you ask for, it will be done for you by my Father in heaven. For where two or three come together in my name, there am I with them. (Matthew 18:15–20)

Phillip Lewis adapts the following process, originally presented by M. Rush in *Management: A Biblical Approach* (1987):[152]

A SCRIPTURAL APPROACH TO CONFRONTATION

1. Deal with facts, not guesses or hearsay.[153] Conflict provides an excellent opportunity to serve others.[154]
2. Make the initial confrontation in private between you and the person involved.[155] Be committed to resolving the conflict quickly. The longer it continues, the more difficult it is to resolve.

---

[152] Myron Rush, *Management: A Biblical Approach* (Wheaton, Ill.: Victor, 1987), 212–215.

[153] Deuteronomy 19:15.

[154] Matthew 5:40–41.

[155] Proverbs 4:25; Matthew 18:15.

Take the initiative in confronting those involved. Do not wait for those involved to approach you.

3. If the other person involved refuses to resolve the conflict, take someone with you and try again.[156] Even though hostility and anger may be present, avoid angry arguments.[157]

4. If the person continues to resist resolving the conflict, you may need to dissolve the relationship.[158]

5. If the other person is willing to repent and correct the problem, forgive him or her and continue the relationship—no matter how often conflicts continue to occur (Luke 17:3–4).[159]

Lewis goes on to say that "change and conflict must be accepted as continuing results of people living, working, and worshipping together. Resolution of conflict by confrontation is a sensible solution for a more productive [ministry] environment, particularly during periods of change."

PRINCIPLES FOR CONFLICT MANAGEMENT

G. Douglas Lewis, in *Resolving Church Conflicts* (1981),[160] identifies seven basic principles for conflict management.

1. Help others feel better about themselves. Persons and organizations manage conflict best when they are feeling good about themselves.

2. Strive for effective communication. Effective communication consists of in-depth and reflective listening and sending, with the knowledge that one's perceptions and messages are uniquely one's own.

---

[156] Matthew 18:16.

[157] Proverbs 14:29.

[158] Matthew 18:17.

[159] Luke 17:3–4.

[160] G. Douglas Lewis, *Resolving Church Conflicts: A Case Study Approach for Local Congregations* (HarperCollins, 1981).

3. Examine and filter assumptions. Unexamined assumptions contribute to destructive conflict.

4. Identify goals; what is wanted. Identifying what a person, group, or organization is trying to accomplish—what is wanted—in a situation is an essential element in conflict management.

5. Identify the primary issues. Until the primary issue has been identified and acknowledged by the principal parties in the conflict, it is difficult to manage the conflict.

6. Develop alternatives for goal achievement. Search for alternatives that will allow all parties to achieve that which is important and fulfilling to them.

7. Institutionalize conflict management processes. To be effective, conflict management processes must be institutionalized and not solely for special occasions.

Ken Sande, in *The Peacemaker* (2004),[161] uses the following principles to guide his approach to resolving conflicts. He calls it the Four G's.

Glorify God. "So, whether you eat or drink or whatever you do, do it all for the glory of God."[162] Biblical peacemaking is motivated and guided by a deep desire to bring honor to God by revealing the reconciling love and power of Jesus Christ.

Get the log out of your eye. "You hypocrite; first take the plank out of your own eye, and then you will see clearly to remove the speck from your brother's eye."[163] When we overlook others' minor offenses and honestly admit our own faults, our opponents will often respond in kind.

Gently restore. "Brothers, if someone is caught in a sin, you who are spiritual should restore him gently. But watch yourself, or you also may be tempted."[164] The goal is to encourage repentance and restore peace.

---

[161] Ken Sande, *The Peacemaker: A Biblical Guide to Resolving Personal Conflict* (Aida: Baker Publishing Group, 2004).

[162] 1 Corinthians 10:31.

[163] Matthew 7:5.

[164] Galatians 6:1.

Go and be reconciled. "Leave your gift there in front of the altar. First go and be reconciled to your brother; then come and offer your gift."[165] Peacemaking involves a commitment to restoring damaged relationships and negotiating just agreements.

CONFLICT MANAGEMENT STYLES

Speed B. Leas wrote a very helpful monograph titled *Discover Your Conflict Management Style* (1998).[166] Generally, conflict management styles include the following approaches or a variation of the following approaches:

PERSUADING

The strategies are those where a person or group attempts to change another's point of view, way of thinking, feelings, or ideas. This approach assumes that the other is incorrect or ignorant and needs to be changed to improve the situation, the relationship, the organization, or the individual.

In using this approach, the "persuader" should be for something rather than against something. Do not interrupt, and do not hurry to make your points. Cover one point at a time, know your key points, and keep coming back to them.

Persuasion should be used only when there is medium to high trust, you have prestige and competence in the other's eyes, goals are compatible, the other perceives that you respect and appreciate him/her, and the other is open to your advice.

COMPELLING

This approach employs the use of physical or emotional force, authority, or pressure to oblige or constrain one party to do something another party alone wants.

---

165   Matthew 5:24.

166   Speed B. Leas, *Discover Your Conflict Management Style* (Rowman & Littlefield Publishers, 1998).

Such an approach may be acceptable when issues of safety, health, or influence may cause pain, damage, or abuse. More subtle application of this approach may be warranted when the mission, vision, beliefs, values, or strategic objectives are in jeopardy, if the person or persons do not comply. If the good order of the ministry or organization is threatened, such an approach may be necessary.

Compelling should be used infrequently—when you or others are being threatened or attacked, when rights are being violated, when you have tacit or explicit authority to demand compliance, when you can call in authority, when the other believes you will use your authority, when there is an inadequate time to work through the differences, when and where all other means have failed, when one is able to monitor performance, when performance is easily evaluated and can be evaluated promptly, and on important or unpopular courses of action.

If this approach is used too frequently, leadership backlash may be encountered. Subversive opposition may be experienced. In the long term, compelling is "caustic and rots out relationships and organizations." Continued compliance will happen only when sanctions are still in existence.

AVOIDANCE

This approach and the correlated approaches of ignoring, accommodating, or fleeing generally are passive-aggressive means in conflict management. In each case, the problem is not fully resolved but remains as a festering influence on the team.

There are, however, some legitimate reasons to consider such approaches—when the cost of working out the problem is greater than the value of having worked it through, when relationships are fragile and insecure, when people need time or space to cool down, when there is conflict on many fronts, when the differences are trivial or irrelevant, when the parties are unable or unwilling to work the issues through but must still work together, when the relationship is not critical to the issue, or when you are powerless to effect change of any kind.

The problem, however, simply will fester overtime and lose its clarity for resolution when other problems cloud and confuse the initial situation. Growth and maturity may be hindered. Things will remain as they are until they are dealt with.

COLLABORATION

This approach is often touted as the best but may only be effective when both parties are willing to work together for a solution. Choosing collaborative strategies requires parties willing to play by collaborative rules.

Such an approach requires joint acknowledgement that there is a problem, agreement on ground rules, agreement on process for dealing with the problem, agreement on the definition of the problem, identification of shared interests, invention of options for mutual gain, agreement on criteria for choosing among the options, and agreement that the option will be jointly chosen.

Dichotomous issues, conflicts over limited resources, high-conflict settings, fear and distrust, and individual predilections are strong enough to derail the process. All preclude the use of collaboration.

Having said that, collaboration often produces high motivation. The quality of decisions is usually significantly increased, people's problem-solving abilities are usually strengthened, and participants are encouraged that they accomplished something formidable together.

NEGOTIATION

This approach refers to a strategy that is like collaboration, except that the expectations of the parties are lower. Instead of seeking solutions that are mutually fulfilling, they hope to get as much as they can of their own preferences.

Negotiation is best used when problem resolution seems negotiable. Some issues are not negotiable, especially when personal beliefs and values are at stake. To negotiate, the prize must be divisible so that each party to the negotiation stands to win something. Negotiation is often a good compromise between collaboration and compelling. All parties must be willing to negotiate. Great power disparity between the negotiating parties may eliminate this approach as an option. Some degree of safety and possibility of approaching the problem rationally—with a clear head and without paralyzing fear—must be present to negotiate effectively.

In using negotiation, the solutions may appear to satisfy but in fact are often less than what was expected when negotiations began. Parties often must be reminded of their agreements after they have been made. Second, the parties might look for loopholes or chances to revise the arrangement to secure a better outcome than originally acquired.

SUPPORT

The major assumption of this strategy is that the other person is the one with the problem and responsibility for fixing it. It is also used when the parties in conflict attempt to triangulate a third person into the mix or to take a side. In this case, the object is to provide support to the other parties to help them resolve it themselves, without providing the solution.

A better way to classify this approach may be to call it a strengthening, encouraging, empowering, or emboldening strategy. The best procedure is to make neutral statements, ask questions, and reflect the content of the conflicting parties, helping them to explore other possible solutions or adapt to the realities of a given conflictive situation. This strategy may also be employed when underlying tensions are the real conflict, rather than the declared specifics.

A possible problem with this strategy may be that it results in ill will that you didn't take the side of the person soliciting your help. He/she may have hoped for more advocacy on his/her behalf. The best outcome will be that the parties in conflict are encouraged to be more responsible for themselves. A support strategy encourages independence and discourages dependence.

CONFLICT RESOLUTION PROCESS

Ken Sande, in *The Peacemaker: A Biblical Guide to Resolving Personal Conflict* (2004), suggests a five-step process for resolving conflicts. He uses the acronym PAUSE.[167]

P—Prepare. Pray, get the facts, identify issues and interests, study the Bible, develop options, anticipate reactions, plan an alternative to a negotiated agreement, select an appropriate time and place to talk, plan your opening remarks, and seek counsel.

A—Affirm relationships. Offer concrete affirmations of the relationship that are legitimate and not manipulative. Demonstrate concern and respect as follows: communicate in a courteous manner, spend time on personal issues, submit to authority, earnestly seek to understand, look out for the interests of others, address sin in a gracious manner, allow face-saving, give praise and thanks.

U—Understand interests. Hear out the other party or parties. Listen carefully to their concerns. Repeat back their concerns to make sure they are heard. State your own interests clearly. Avoid using emotional language. Clarify underlying policies and procedures if they are relevant. Review previous agreements.

S—Search for creative solutions. Practice spontaneous inventing. Brainstorm possible solutions together. Avoid providing a solution at first. Avoid the assumption that there is only one solution. Explain the benefits of each possible solution that warrants consideration. Incorporate policies and procedures that apply to the solution(s).

E—Evaluate options objectively and reasonably. Refer to relevant biblical principles. Introduce appropriate facts, official rules and regulations, and operating limitations and restrictions. Seek advice from experts, respected advisers, and affected personnel, if needed. Consider other ministries or internal/external systems that may be impacted by the option.

Conflict will always be a part of human interactions and relationships.

---

[167] Ken Sande, *The Peacemaker: A Biblical Guide to Resolving Personal Conflict* (Aida: Baker Publishing Group, 2004), 227–245.

Learning how to effectively resolve conflict is a necessary leadership skill. Matthew 18:15–20 gives us a biblical approach to resolving conflicts. The Bible is full of principles for resolving such conflicts.

Resolving conflicts is rarely an enjoyable process until resolution is acquired. Then, all that proceeded in coming to a solution is worth the anguish of getting there.

QUESTIONS TO PONDER

With whom are you presently in conflict?
What will you do to resolve the conflict?
What process will you use to resolve the conflict?

RECOMMENDED RESOURCE

The Peacemaker: A Biblical Guide to Resolving Personal Conflict (2004) by Ken Sande

MOTIVATING (HOW TO MOTIVATE PEOPLE TO EXCEL)

You may see yourself as a teacher or a facilitator, but some of you may not see yourself as a leader. Yet in everyday life you lead or follow, sometimes moving between the two several times in a given day. When you take initiative to motivate (or influence) a follower to do something, you are exercising leadership. When you provide direction or guidance to others, you are exercising leadership.

In a rather simplistic sense, people are led; things are managed. When definitions of leadership are reviewed, one common theme emerges—influence. In the New Testament, we are encouraged to influence others for Christ. So you may be a leader by nature, a leader by training, or even a reluctant leader, *but* you are a leader nevertheless.

One of the primary leadership functions of a leader is being able to motivate others to excel at what they do. One of the best ways to motivate others is to adjust your leadership of them to their current capacity and capability, and then lead them in to realizing the potential within them.

Over the last few decades, people in the field of management have been involved in a search for a best style of leadership. Research clearly indicates that there is no single all-purpose leadership style. Effective and successful leaders are those who can adapt their behaviors to meet the demands of unique situations.

To that end, I believe one of the best models for leading others and helping them reach their God-ordained potential is the Situational Leadership model, first popularized by Ken Blanchard, who originally developed Situational Leadership with Paul Hersey at Ohio University in 1968. It gained prominence in 1969 in their classic text, *Management of Organizational Behavior* (2012), now in its tenth edition.[168]

The Situational Leadership model, however, is not only suitable for any organization; it is ideally suited for ministry. I would also recommend it as a parenting model applied to raising children. I have adapted the model and call it *situational engagement*.

The model focuses on the individuals being led considering their capabilities, limitations, and weaknesses. It meets them where they are and moves them in a direction that helps them realize their God-given potential, related to specific assigned tasks and their successful completion. The leader becomes the servant and adapts his or her approach based on the readiness of the person or group being led. Effective use of this model depends on the flexibility of the leader and the willingness of the follower to be led. It is others oriented and supports biblical principles of justice, mercy, and fair play.

The model suggests leadership engagement patterns. They are referred to by various descriptors. For me, telling, selling, participating, and delegating does not adequately summarize the real nature of each function. I prefer, instead, to call them director (S1), coach (S2), supporter (S3) and observer/mentor (S4).

---

[168] Paul Hersey, Kenneth H. Blanchard, and Dewey E. Johnson, *Management of Organizational Behavior*, 10th edition (London: Pearson Education, 2012).

Four Engagement Patterns

DIRECTOR	COACH	SUPPORTER	OBSERVER
Telling	Selling	Participating	Delegating
Guiding	Explaining	Encouraging	Mentoring
Directing	Clarifying	Collaborating	Monitoring
Establishing	Persuading	Assisting	Evaluating

Although we may exhibit a *predominant* style we should not limit our role to that style alone because it does not fit the changing levels of readiness experienced by those we lead. If we fixate on one style over the others, we will encourage our followers to fixate on one readiness level and discourage them from moving on to progressively more independent performances.

Instead, we must learn to adapt and adopt different roles for different situations and different readiness levels. Flexibility of the leader, in this case, will serve him or her well in motivating others. I believe God has called us to be thermostats, not thermometers. We should set the environmental temperature of our field of engagement, rather than simply reflecting the temperature of the environment.

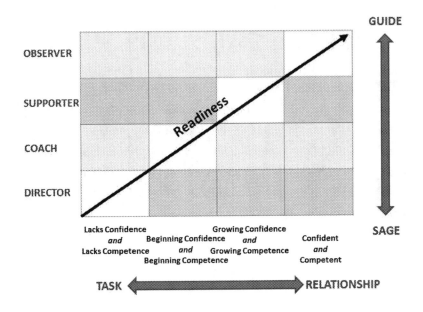

The director (S1) leadership style is appropriate when a person being led lacks competence and confidence and is unable, unwilling, or insecure about completing a given task or fulfilling a given role. In this case, provision of specific instructions and close supervision of performance is warranted. The whys and wherefores are not usually offered by the leader in this phase. The leader generally makes all the decisions; the follower carries out the directions.

The coach (S2) leadership style is appropriate when a person begins to be confident and competent, even though he or she may still be unable to do it themselves but are now willing or more confident about completing the task or fulfilling an assigned role. In this situation, the leader explains his or her decision or decisions and provides clarification as needed. The leader still makes the final decision but encourages dialogue and explanations behind the decision. He or she may ask how the follower would handle the situation, if given complete authority to do so.

The supporter (S3) leadership style would be appropriate when a follower is growing in his or her competence and confidence and is able but still may be a bit unwilling or insecure about doing it or functioning on his or her own, regarding the task or role. Decisions in this case are made conjointly between leader and follower or in some cases by the follower with encouragement and support from the leader. Ideas are shared openly by the leader and the follower, with the initiative moving toward the follower.

In the last stage, the leader assumes the role of observer/mentor (S4), as the follower shows both confidence and competence and is able and willing to perform the task or handle the role with little or no supervision. The leader delegates responsibility for decisions and actual implementation to the follower. The follower now makes all the decisions and may seek advice from the mentor as needed.

The leader should not wait until the follower is completely ready for the next style of leadership approach. Instead, the leader should move to the next style when the follower shows signs he/she is moving in that direction. In other words, the follower may lag a bit, but the leader should move ahead slowly anyway. Stress and/or tension is to be expected and is good, even though the follower may not be completely ready to move to the next stage.

The chart above summarizes the model in terms of the situational dynamics, who makes decisions, what leadership approach is appropriate, and the readiness level indicators that will help to determine which leadership style will be most effective.

I have learned over time that teaching (or parenting or leading) is situational—the style or approach changes in each situation, set of circumstances, or events encountered along the way. Sometimes God calls us to be a sage on the stage, while in other situations he calls us to be a guide by the side. When should we be a sage on the stage, and when should we be a guide by the side? It depends on the readiness of those being taught. Generally, a director or coach is a sage on the stage, while supporter and observer/mentor are guides by the side.

Readiness is a measure of willingness, ability, and security. The degree to which our followers are willing, able, and secure will determine the type of engagement needed to help them become mature and confident in what will be demanded of them as they seek to find their way in the world. A leader should adjust his or her leading according to the readiness of the follower for a given task, circumstance, or event he or she faces during the developmental years of life.

If your follower has never led a project team, don't tell him or her, "Make it happen." Likewise, in the home, if your son has never cut the lawn, don't say, "The mower is in the garage; go to it." That's a formula for disaster.

If your follower has successfully led project teams, don't tell him or her how to lead a team. If your daughter has confidence and has shown competence in riding a bike, don't force her to listen to repeated directions from you on how to ride a bike.

In a more personal application, let's look at a situation between a father and son. A son has taken an interest in building model planes. Having never done it before, a father would build one as the son watched. He would provide step-by-step directions as director. He operates as a sage on the stage.

As the son shows a willingness to try to build a model and demonstrates beginning competence and confidence but is still unable to do it on his own, the father would coach the son. Once the son showed some ability, as evidenced by a growing competence and confidence, but still is a bit insecure, the father would assume the role of supporter, and they would build the model together. At this point, he would shift to a guide by the side.

Finally, when the son shows he is confident and competent, willing, able, and secure, the father would shift to being an observer, still engaged but at a distance. When needed, he would offer his advice as a mentor. He becomes a mentor, only offering advice when asked, while the son builds the model himself.

I hope you see the application of situational engagement. All leaders operate from a default leadership style, either director, coach, supporter, or observer/mentor. The key is to be flexible and adaptable to change your leadership style to accommodate the level of readiness of those being led.

To learn your default leadership style and how to become an

effective situational leader, I recommend you visit the Ken Blanchard Companies.[169] Instruments and other helpful resources are available to assist you and those you lead in becoming better leaders, using the Situational Leadership model. Another excellent resource is *The Situational Leader* (1997) by Paul Hersey.[170] Although written in 1985, it contains timeless truths on leading and effective leadership. Likewise, *Leadership and the One Minute Manager* is another excellent resource. On the back cover are the following remarks:

> Leadership and the One Minute Manager teaches leaders the world-renowned method of developing self-reliance in those they manage: Situational Leadership® II. In Leadership and the One Minute Manager, you'll learn why adapting leadership styles to team members based on their key goals and tasks is so important and why knowing when to delegate, support, or direct is critical. By consistently using Situational Leadership® II's proven model and powerful techniques, leaders can develop and retain competent, motivated, confident employees. This remarkable, easy-to-follow book is a priceless guide to personalized leadership that elicits the best performance from your team—and the best bottom line for any business.[171]

QUESTIONS TO PONDER

Which leadership style is your dominant style?

---

[169] Ken Blanchard Companies, https://www.kenblanchard.com/Products-Services/Situational-Leadership-II.

[170] Paul Hersey, *The Situational Leader* (Escondido: Center for Leadership Studies, 1997).

[171] Ken Blanchard, Patricia Zigarmi, and Drea Zigarmi, *Leadership and the One Minute Manager: Increasing Effectiveness Through Situational Leadership® II* (New York: HarperCollins, 2013), front cover flap.

How adaptable and flexible are you regarding your style?

How could those you lead benefit from situational engagement?

RECOMMENDED RESOURCE

Leadership and the One Minute Manager Updated Edition: Increasing Effectiveness Through Situational Leadership II (2013) by Ken Blanchard, Patricia Zigarmi, and Drea Zigarmi

INFLUENCING (HOW TO FOCUS ON WHAT YOU CAN INFLUENCE)

We operate within two circles—the circle of concern and the circle of influence.

**Circle of Concern
(Things we cannot
personally change)**

**Circle of Influence
(Things we can
personally change)**

Within the circle of concern are issues we are concerned about, but we have little or no control over the issues that fall within this sphere. For instance, we might be concerned about political or economic issues in Washington, a judge's ruling on an issue that touches us, a decision being made by someone regarding our circumstances, world poverty, global warming, or any host of matters that cause us concern. We may have a limited influence on these matters, but for all practical purposes, they are out of our reach to do anything about them. In these cases, we have essentially one option—prayer. Once we have prayed about these matters, we must release them to the Lord and move on to those issues we can control.

Within the circle of influence are issues over which we have some degree of control. Our direct input or interaction will determine the outcome of these issues. People, events, and circumstances can be changed by our direct involvement. Our influence may be of a direct nature or indirect nature. Our direct influence will address the specific issue directly. Our indirect influence may be to interact with factors that may impact the situation indirectly (e.g., a note to a friend or authority may cause that friend or authority to respond to a set of circumstances over which he/she has some influence). Organizational influence is the effect we wield and how we affect a situation as we carry out our obligations, responsibilities, and duties in our vocation. Opportunities will present themselves when we can alter the direction of a strategy, process, methodology, practice, or project by influencing the outcome.

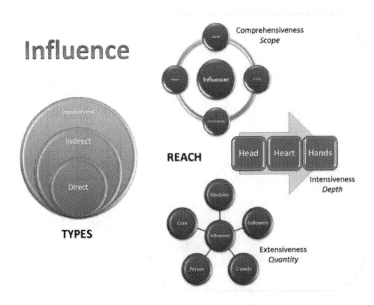

As we properly steward our influence, it will grow comprehensively, intensively, and extensively. Abuse our influence, and it will shrink in terms of reach. Comprehensive growth should do with the audiences we influence. These domains may include people, causes, events, and circumstances. Intensive growth relates to the depth with which we penetrate the lives of those being influenced. We not only stimulate the intellect but affect the emotions and passion of our circle. We can compel action. Extensive growth represents the quantity of those affected by our influence. The scope could extend from a person, to a core of people, to disciples, followers, and crowds. The size expands proportionately to the influence we wield. Our sphere of influence could include any of the following activities or roles:

Direct	Indirect	Organizational
Individuals	Committee	Supervisor
Small groups	Advisory board	Program director
Project team	Executive board	Department head
Ministries	Writing	Organization head
Seminars	Radio/TV/internet	Policy formulator
Conferences	Networking	Board member
Mentoring	Supporting	Sponsoring
Counseling	Blogging	Resourcing
Advising	Social networks	Vision casting

Each of us has a finite amount of energy at our disposal (emotional, spiritual, and physical). The extent of that energy will differ for each person. Our circle of influence can expand as we grow emotionally, spiritually, and intellectually—it can also diminish through bad decisions and/or sin in our lives.

If we expend our limited energy on matters over which we have little influence or control, the energy remaining will be reduced. When we turn our attention to issues within our sphere of influence, we will find that the circle of influence has shrunk, while our circle of concern has grown. Spending our finite energy in this sphere will only increase our anxiety and stress because we can do little to change the outcome.

Focusing our finite energy primarily on issues within our circle of influence and praying about issues within our circle of concern (and releasing these issues to the Lord) will reduce the circle of concern to a more manageable size and therefore cause less anxiety and stress in our lives. This is a far more constructive activity—focusing on what we can change and leaving for God those issues we cannot change to any significant degree.

Making an issue of every issue will soon diminish our influence. What we say on a given issue will be discounted because we make an issue of every issue. Choose your issues carefully if you want to influence the outcome.

Focus on your circle of influence and pray about your circle of concern.

QUESTIONS TO PONDER

What falls within your circle of concern?
What falls within your circle of influence?
What issues are you making an issue that shouldn't be an issue?

RECOMMENDED RESOURCE

Impact Your Sphere of Influence: Bringing God's Presence in the Workplace (2013) by Linda Fields

MOBILIZING (HOW TO MOBILIZE A TEAM TO MEET ANY CHALLENGE)

This competency—mobilizing a team—is crucial for many reasons. Ministry is not accomplished alone but in community with others who are committed to the same vision and objectives. We can accomplish far more together than we can individually. The complexity of ministry today demands the focused efforts of like-minded individuals, headed in the same direction together.

In *Doing Church as a Team*, Wayne Cordeiro (2004) makes the following points:

> Each one of us has been given a gift, a calling. Each of us has a place or a role to fill. (Each of us has) a unique thumbprint, our own individual circuitry, designed by God himself. He places each of us in a community ... with a divine purpose. He fits us alongside others who have a similar assignment and calls us a family, a team, the Church. No one person is meant to carry out this

assignment alone; it was designed that way. We were created to do church as a team.[172]

A CASE FOR MINISTRY TEAMS

Dr. Jerry Sheveland, former president of the Converge (previously Baptist General Conference) and I, former vice president of operations and strategic initiatives for Bethel Seminary, developed a manual titled *Empowering Leaders for a Disciple-Making Church* (1992), while ministering together in a large church in California. Several insights related to ministry teams follow:

FOUNDATION FOR MINISTRY TEAMS

Social research and organizational practices have established the validity of teamwork. When workers are gathered into teams that make decisions together, encourage one another, set course goals, and work together, good things happen. Product quality improves. Worker pride and ownership increases. Innovations emerge. Job satisfaction is observably strengthened as well.

The Bible gives us many examples of using the team approach. Several models of ministry teams emerge.[173]

- Moses. The great prophet Moses is often used as an example of effective delegation. This is because he followed his father-in-law's advice to develop a system of judges. What also must be seen is that his team of officials was so organized that for every ten Israelites, there was a leader. This made it possible for a large nation to operate as a huge network of small groups.[174]
- Nehemiah. The rebuilding of Jerusalem's walls under the leadership of Nehemiah is perhaps the Bible's best management

---

[172] Wayne Cordeiro, *Doing Church as a Team* (Bloomington: Bethany House Publishers, 2004), 8–9.

[173] Jerry Sheveland and Greg Bourgond, *Empowering Leaders for a Disciple-Making Church* (San Diego: College Avenue Baptist Church, 1992), 2-9 and 2-10.

[174] Exodus 18:1–26.

case study. Nehemiah describes how organized teams of workers took responsibility to rebuild various portions of the wall. Team after team surrounded the city, each doing their part to fulfill Nehemiah's God-given vision.[175]

- Jesus. The primary method of Christ's leadership was to mentor a team of twelve men to establish his church. Interestingly, when the Lord sent these men out on ministry assignments, it was never as individuals. He sent them out as teams of two or more.[176]

- Paul. Except for Jesus, Paul may have been the most effective leader in the history of the church. He, too, mentored individuals into ministry teams. Everywhere he went to plant churches, he brought a team with him. That's why at the end of many of his epistles, he sent greetings from team members ministering with him. Also, when churches were planted, Paul instructed that elders (a team of leaders) were to be appointed.[177]

- Early church. Perhaps the most convincing biblical example is the organization of the early church. It was structured as a network of house churches. So the very nature of the church was circles of people nurturing each other and serving the Lord together.

MINISTRY TEAM OBJECTIVES

Once again, Dr. Jerry Sheveland helps to clarify the meaning of ministry teams. The leader has two objectives in building a ministry team: (1) team relationships committed to mutual encouragement and spiritual nurture, and (2) team functions committed to integrating each member's spiritual gifts for fulfilling a shared task within the larger mission of the church.

---

[175] Nehemiah 3:1–32.
[176] Luke 10:1.
[177] Luke 4:7–15; Titus 1:5.

MINISTRY TEAM COMPONENTS

Dr. Sheveland identifies four ministry team components using the acrostic TEAM.[178]

T—Every team must be built on *trust*. Trust is the cornerstone of the relationships of all the members. Trust opens the door for vulnerability, truth telling, caring and nurturing. It is the foundation of effective communication. It can only be achieved as we allow ourselves to grow in the understanding of what Jesus meant when he said, "By this shall all men know that you are my disciples that you have love for one another." Trust, on the one hand, means that a team member seeks to be trustworthy and therefore is open to spiritual life examination and encouragement in the community of other believers. Trust also means that each team member believes in fellow team members and seeks to encourage them in the fulfillment of relationships and ministry tasks.

E—Every team *experiences* spiritual giftedness in Christ. It is true that God gifts every believer. By extension, it must also be true that God gifts communities of believers—that is, churches—to accomplish specific tasks based on the fulfillment of those gifts (and the purposes God has for that church or ministry organization). It is important that every believer seek to discover the spiritual gift (or gifts) that God has entrusted to him or her. Knowing and understanding one's spiritual gifts helps to focus the believer's attention on that which God has called him or her to do. The list of what we are capable of doing is usually longer than the list of what we are called to do. Focusing on that which God has called us to accomplish helps to bring clarity to ministry tasks. Therefore, in a team of people, it is essential that team members are on their individual as well as corporate spiritual life adventures, discovering and actualizing their spiritual giftedness.

A—God calls us to be *accountable*. In the context of being part of a team, accountability has many facets. There is relational accountability both to God and to other team members. There is also functional

---

[178] Jerry Sheveland and Greg Bourgond, *Empowering Leaders for a Disciple-Making Church* (San Diego: College Avenue Baptist Church, 1992), 2-7 and 2-8.

accountability in terms of ministry responsibilities. In the context of any spiritually motivated team, members are accountable relationally before God and care deeply about the spiritual growth and ministry success of each other. It can truthfully be said that every team member must care more about the other member's ministry success than he does about his own and therefore will seek to do everything to encourage spiritual, relational, and functional accountability. The exercise of accountability without the foundation of trust may result in speaking truth, but where accountability is exercised within the context of a trust relationship, it becomes "speaking the truth in love," which is the biblical model and our mandate.

M—Creative *methodologies* are employed. The methods that a team uses are important. The methods are a direct result of the exercise of the spiritual giftedness God has entrusted to team members. Emphasis on methods alone should never precede trust relationships and spiritual giftedness because people are more important than program. People and the gifts God has given them should determine programs. There is no limit to the kinds of creative methods that can be employed. All methods, however, are subject to the standards of biblical doctrine. The timeless truth of God's Word must be conveyed using timely methodologies if we are to reach our culture for Christ. Methodologies should be the means to an end, not an end in themselves.

FUNCTIONS IN MOBILIZING MINISTRY TEAMS

There are six primary functions in mobilizing a ministry team: planning, recruitment, training, resourcing, supervision, and evaluation.

1. Planning: The first step in mobilizing a ministry team is planning. The following questions should be answered: What is the purpose of the ministry team? Every team must have a clearly defined purpose for existing. The purpose of the team should be tied to one or more key objectives of the ministry plan. For instance, let's assume that a church believes that every member is a minister and should have ministry. Let us further assume that the church has an objective of engaging 75 percent

of its members in some form of ministry within the first year of becoming a member of the church. One or more ministry teams will be needed to meet this objective.

Who will lead the team? A leader should be recruited to lead the team. An effective team leader can function well in four distinct dimensions of team leadership: vision casting, nurturing, managing, and mentoring.

2. Vision casting: For the team to work together effectively, the members must share a common vision. The leader's role is to first guide the team in identifying and articulating a shared vision—a vision that does not contradict the overall vision of the church or ministry agency but operates within its framework. Second, the leader is to embody the vision with passion. Third, the leader must help the team translate the vision into long-term objectives and short-term goals. Finally, the leader must be able to communicate the vision repeatedly.

3. Nurturing: The significant uniqueness of the ministry team leader is the strong emphasis on the nurture component. The team leader nurtures a loving team environment through ample doses of caring, communication, congratulation, and celebration.

4. Managing: Management is the process of working with the team members and their resources to accomplish ministry goals. The management process involves planning, organizing, motivating, and controlling performance and productivity.

5. Mentoring: Perhaps the single greatest factor in building an effective ministry team is the life example of the leader. The leader is a player/coach who mentors team members by modeling and teaching several qualities, including an enthusiastic attitude, spiritual growth and integrity, relational skills, a servant spirit, ministry skills, and believing prayer and perseverance.

Those who have sanctioned the team should develop the profile of the leader (e.g., the board, the pastor, the champion responsible for a strategy in the ministry plan). The profile should include the following considerations: level of spiritual maturity required to lead the team, spiritual gifts required to lead the team, and time commitment required to lead the team.

What functions or activities will the team carry out? For instance, if the purpose of the ministry is to help members identify their spiritual gifts and to provide opportunities within or outside the church to exercise those gifts, then the functions and/or activities might include providing training to help people identify their spiritual gifts and providing placement services to help people find a way to use their gifts. What type of members will be required to carry out the functions of the teams?

Once the purpose of the team has been defined, the leader chosen, and the primary functions identified, then the type and number of members needed to carry out the functions can be determined. Central to this process is the design of ministry descriptions for each member of the team.

A good ministry description answers nine questions. (1) What is the role? (2) What time frame are we talking about? (3) What is our purpose? (4) What is the assignment? (5) What qualifications are needed? (6) What are the responsibilities? (7) What authority will the position entail? (8) Who reports to whom? (9) What training will be needed?

Following our example, several people may be needed: a course designer, an instructor, a host or hostess, a promoter, a connection counselor, etc. Each position will require a ministry description. Each ministry description should include the following elements, the substance of which should be stated on one page of paper, if possible.

- Ministry position title: What is the title of the position? The title should be clear and understandable. There should be no ambiguity, especially if the church or ministry organization uses common terms, such as director, coordinator, assistant, or some other levelized descriptor. If a hierarchy exists, choose the appropriate title to fit the authority and role.

- Functional description: What is the primary function of the position? The description of the role should be one paragraph that describes the primary function of the position. The description should be concise, comprehensive, and clear.

- Qualifications: What are the qualifications necessary to perform the primary functions of the position? In other words, what spiritual gifts are best suited to the position? What passion is required? What skills or competencies are necessary? What talents or education is needed?

- Commitment level: How often will their services be required? Does the position demand daily engagement, or is it a weekly, monthly, or quarterly commitment? Will their services be required periodically, occasionally, or when needed, based on a given situation?

- Term of service: How long will they be required to serve in the position? Is it a six-month term, one year, or three years? It is important to identify a limit so that individuals do not think they are being asked to serve until they drop. Declaring the term of service shows respect for individuals and lets them know that there is a defined end to their service. They certainly can be asked to serve another term. Placing a limit on their service gives the leader an opportunity to replace those who have not performed up to the requirements of the position.

- Responsibilities: What are the responsibilities associated with the position? The responsibilities should be in a bullet list, with each bullet addressing one responsibility only. In other words, do not lump several responsibilities under one bullet. This list should encompass all major responsibilities of the position. The list does not have to be exhaustive.

- Reporting relationships: To whom will the person report? Who will report to the person holding the position? What authority will the person have? Who must he/she liaison with in the performance of his/her duties? What communication is required?

- Support provided: What training will be provided for the position? What resources will be made available to enhance the individuals' performance while they serve in the position? What support will they be given while they serve? If you are asking someone to walk the high wire of service, you should provide a safety net of support. People are more willing to serve when they know they will be trained and supported.

Once these questions are answered and position descriptions have been developed, the selection process can begin.

RECRUITMENT

Recruitment for ministry team members is distinct from recruiting a worker to fulfill a designated task. The leader is offering the opportunity to be mentored by a proven leader as a member of a team committed to mutual encouragement and serving God together. Recruitment is more like a proposal of marriage than hiring a maid. It operates on a belief that God has already prepared certain people for the tasks he wants accomplished. Our part is to assist that divine transaction as a loving leader who is more interested in the person than the task.

Two objectives of recruiting team members are operational: (1) Demonstrate love for the individuals by offering to invest in them. (2) Assist the fulfillment of the church's mission by matching a person's spiritual giftedness and ministry passions with a suitable team.

The primary recruiter for the ministry team should be the person leading the team. If the leader inherits members from an existing team, he or she should reinterview those members to ensure the right fit for the intended purposes of the ministry team. Repurposing existing members is essential for positive team dynamics and interactions.

The recruitment process modeled by Jesus is ideal for our purposes. The following eight steps are recommended for the leader of the ministry team:

1. Alignment. Understand your mission, vision, and objectives first. As a leader, your primary task is to equip people for ministry by reproducing yourself in them. Jesus said to his disciples, "As the Father has sent Me, I am sending you."[179]

2. Networking. Establish or find settings where you can observe and begin relationships with people who may be potential team members. These "fishing pools" may include your Sunday school class, previous ministry teams, graduates from various training courses, recommendations from respected advisers, your small group, etc.

   One day as Jesus was standing by the Lake of Gennesaret, with the people crowding around him and listening to the Word of God, he saw at the water's edge two boats left there by the fishermen, who were washing their nets. He got into one of the boats, the one belonging to Simon, and asked him to put out a little from shore. Then he sat down and taught the people from the boat.[180]

3. Prayer. Establish uninterrupted time to pray. Ask the Lord to lead you to those he wants you to approach. Resist the temptation to select people who are already overcommitted or are everyone's best choice. We tend to go after the people who have proven themselves in the past. You may need to look at people who do not have a proven track record—emerging leaders.

   One of those days Jesus went out to a mountainside to pray and spent the night praying to God. When morning came, he called his disciples to him and chose twelve of them, whom he also designated apostles.[181]

4. Approach. Personally approach the people God puts on your heart. Don't recruit by newsletter, by mail, or by phone. In a positive setting, sit down and explore the potential team relationship with the person. Jesus did this one on one. As he

---

[179] John 20:21.
[180] Luke 5:1–3.
[181] Luke 6:12–13.

walked along, he saw Levi, son of Alphaeus, sitting at the tax collector's booth. "Follow me," Jesus told him, and Levi got up and followed him.[182]

5. Envisioning. Share your vision and passion. People are not encouraged to serve by coercive pressure or guilt. People are inspired to serve when a compelling vision is presented. Also share the cost of becoming a member of the team. Let them know the part they will play and how important they are to achieving God's purposes.

   "Then he called the crowd to him along with his disciples and said: 'If anyone would come after me, he must deny himself and take up his cross and follow me. For whoever wants to save his life will lose it, but whoever loses his life for me and for the gospel will save it.'"[183]

6. Challenge. Offer them something greater than the task. Offer them a calling, and challenge them to set aside lesser things. Always treat people as God's special gifts and not as functionaries. Be proper stewards of his resources. "Come, follow me, Jesus said, and I will make you fishers of men. At once they left their nets and followed him."[184]

7. Support. Assure them of your ongoing support, encouragement, and investment in their lives. Deliver on your support. Illustrate how you have done so in the past, if that is the case. You should be prepared to identify the ways in which you will support them (e.g., resourcing, training, barrier removal, buffer, etc.). Before God the Father, Jesus said about his team, "While I was with them I protected them, and kept them safe."[185]

8. Multiplication. Enlist those who are already team members to approach others in their circle of relationships. Philip found Nathanael and told him, "We have found the one Moses wrote

---

[182] Mark 2:14.
[183] Mark 8:34–36.
[184] Matthew 4:9–20.
[185] John 17:12.

about in the Law, and about whom the prophets also wrote—
Jesus of Nazareth, the son of Joseph."[186]

PURPOSING

Each person should understand what his or her unique role and
responsibilities are as a member of the ministry team. The leader also
must articulate how their unique contributions combine to produce the
desired results related to their purposes and goals.

Earlier, we mentioned that for the team to work together effectively,
the members must share a common vision. The leader's role is first to
guide the team in identifying and articulating a shared vision—a vision
that does not contradict the overall vision of the church or ministry
agency but operates within its framework. Second, the leader is to
embody the vision with passion. Third, the leader must help the team
translate the vision into long-term objectives and short-term goals.
Finally, the leader must be able to communicate the vision frequently.

TRAINING

Considerable thought should be given to the types of training
opportunities that would benefit team members, individually and
as a group. For each member to perform at his/her best, preservice
training may have to be arranged. If you are asking individuals to fulfill
responsibilities unfamiliar to them, then essential training must be
provided. To maintain their effectiveness, in-service training might have
to be conducted periodically. In any case, a budget for such training is
important.

Three types of training should be considered: formal, informal,
and nonformal.[187] Dr. J. Robert Clinton gives us helpful definitions
of each. Formal training may include credit or noncredit coursework,
certificate programs, or correspondence courses designed for intensive,

---

[186] John 1:45.

[187] J. Robert Clinton, *Leadership Emergence Theory: A Self-Study Manual for
Analyzing the Development of a Christian Leader* (Altadena: Barnabas Publishers,
1989), 160.

rapid acquisition of knowledge and skills. This may be accomplished through technology-mediated delivery over the internet or by some other means.

Informal training may include being mentored by another who possesses the desired competencies and skills. It may include an apprenticeship under someone who has held the position before. It also may include simple evaluation of existing models, Sunday school classes, and observation or involvement in related or similar ministry tasks.

Nonformal training describes deliberate nonprogrammatic, noninstitutionalized (nonacademic) training that leads to functional skills for ministry. Such training may include seminars, workshops, retreats, focused intensives, and access to specific training resources, such as training manuals on appropriate subjects germane to one's responsibilities on the ministry team.

RESOURCING

One of the most important elements in mobilizing a ministry team is to provide material and financial resources so that the team can carry out their functional responsibilities effectively and efficiently. The leader is responsible for identifying necessary resources, where they can be found, and how they should be allocated. Removing barriers that hinder the team's effectiveness and efficiency is also a part of resourcing.

Simply put, resourcing requirements are determined by answering and responding to the following questions:

- What material resources does the team need?
- What finances will be required to meet the needs of the team?
- What material and financial resources are currently available to the team?
- What resources held by others could be shared with the team?
- Who are the points of contact for needed material and financial resources?
- What barriers should be addressed that may hinder the performance of the team?

SUPERVISION

The leader is responsible for supervising the work of the ministry team. This means that the leader always must be aware of what the team is doing. Understanding expectations and managing those expectations are the keys to successful supervision. The following principles will help a leader become an effective supervisor:

- Know what to expect (i.e., desired results).
- Be observant.
- Be available.
- Be willing to remove barriers.
- Appreciate members' uniqueness.
- Hold people accountable to the results.
- Correct in private; praise in public.
- Be willing to intercede on their behalf.
- Err on the side of grace.
- Celebrate when possible.
- Encourage always.

One of the best models for supervising team members is called the Situational Leadership model. This model is ideally suited for ministry because it focuses on the individuals being led, considering their capabilities, limitations, and weaknesses. It meets them where they are and moves them in a direction that helps them realize their God-given potential. Effective and successful supervision adapts supervisory behavior to meet the demands of unique situations. The leader becomes the servant and adapts his/her approach, based on the readiness of the person or group being led. Effective use of this model depends on the flexibility of the leader and the willingness of the follower to be led. It is others oriented and supports biblical principles of justice, mercy, and fair play.

Effective supervision is accomplished by determining the readiness level of an individual for a specific task and adjusting the type of interaction needed to facilitate the successful performance of his/her responsibilities. Some people need more direction than others, who may need a coach. Still others may need only occasional support, and others simply may need to be released to do what they have been called to do. Micromanagement produces unhealthy dependence or unwelcome intrusion that leads to anger and frustration. Again, a guide by the side is far more effective than a sage on the stage when it comes to effective supervision practices.

EVALUATION

Periodic evaluation of performance is essential to honor the efforts of the team and to improve its performance.

CORRECTING POOR PERFORMANCE

Assessing job performance can be subjective; it need not be. Clear performance criteria help a supervisor objectively evaluate a subordinate's performance. Quarterly SMART (specific, measurable, attainable, results-oriented, and time-constrained) goals are another means of assessing performance.

When an employee's performance consistently falls short of defined expectations, an intervention of sorts must be conducted. Before the actual meeting takes place, the supervisor must collect concrete examples of where performance did not meet declared criteria. Three to four examples should be sufficient.

In the performance review meeting, the supervisor should attempt to ascertain if outside concerns have impeded the individual's performance of late (e.g., health crisis, family crisis, personal crisis). This necessary first step honors individuals by giving them an opportunity to acknowledge issues that have seriously affected how they carry out their responsibilities.

Employees might not admit to an outside influence because they wish to keep it private, or it's an embarrassment to them. If they do acknowledge a legitimate outside influence, that circumstance should inform how the supervisor proceeds.

SIXTY, THIRTY, AND OUT PLAN

If the employee does not admit to a serious impacting circumstance or none indeed exists, then the supervisor should move directly to address the poor performance, using a sixty, thirty, and out plan.

SIXTY-DAY GET-WELL PLAN

When the employee admits that his/her performance has not been up to par, has not satisfied declared expectations, has not been up to standard, or has been unsatisfactory (this is essential), a sixty-day get-well plan should be prepared. The employee must write the plan in accordance with defined criteria from the supervisor. For instance, the plan should include SMART goals with quantifiable or qualitative measurement criteria that will provide unmistakable proof that performance is back on par. The plan should include periodic meetings with the supervisor over the ninety-day period to assess progress and adjustment, as necessary.

When it becomes clear to the supervisor that the plan, as implemented, will not improve performance to a satisfactory level, then a thirty-day get-well plan should be implemented.

THIRTY-DAY GET-WELL PLAN

The supervisor should explain why the employee's plan has failed to yield the desired results. At this point, it does not matter if the employee agrees with the assessment. The supervisor now writes a thirty-day get-well plan, to which the employee must comply. The desired results must be very specific and detailed so that there is no room for dispute. At this point, the employee is told if he/she does not successfully turn his/her performance around to meet declared expectations, disciplinary action will follow that might include one or more of the following actions (or any other options, at the disposal of the supervisor, in accordance with the organization's established polices, practices, and procedures):

- Letter of reprimand
- Pay reduction

- Demotion
- Reassignment
- Termination

The disciplinary action must be carried out quickly.

REGULAR MEETINGS

Regular scheduled meetings are helpful to plan activities, report progress, mediate problems, and celebrate victories. These meetings should not be too frequent or infrequent. Monthly meetings are recommended, unless the project timeline demands otherwise. In other words, preparation activities may only require monthly meetings, while conduct of a program may require biweekly meetings until the program is completed.

STAFF REPORTS

A monthly staff report should be no longer than two pages. It should include the following items:

- Summary of responsibilities,
- Progress toward agreed-upon goals,
- Status of expenditures against budget,
- Accomplishments during the reporting period,
- Concerns (e.g., missed deadlines, barriers encountered, finance needs, etc.),
- Events attendance (if any were scheduled during the reporting period), and
- Prayer requests.

PERFORMANCE APPRAISALS

The leader should conduct semiannual performance appraisals of each member of the ministry team. Leaders often are hesitant to evaluate volunteers. They feel that the volunteer will resent an evaluation. This is a myth. People will rise to expectations, if clearly understood and stated.

People appreciate performance feedback, especially if it is accurate and constructive.

The following areas of evaluation are recommended. The team member should be evaluated as follows:

- Excellent (E): Performance significantly and consistently exceeds the standard.
- Very good (V): Performance exceeds the standard.
- Satisfactory (S): Performance meets the standard.
- Needs improvement (NI): Performance does not meet the standard.
- Not applicable (NA): Does not apply.

Performance categories: The leader should provide an indicator of performance (E, V, S, NI) in each area, supplemented by brief comments, if necessary. Speculation and rumored information regarding a team member's performance should be avoided. Firsthand observations from other team members and performance personally observed by the leader is preferred.

1. Consistently demonstrates a positive attitude
2. Exhibits a growing spiritual maturity
3. Interacts well with other team members
4. Demonstrates interest in learning and improving
5. Accomplishes the essential duties of the position
6. Is responsive to requests for assistance from others
7. Communicates effectively with others
8. Responds positively to suggestions, instructions, or criticisms
9. Takes initiative in taking on responsibility and seeking out information
10. Follows through and demonstrates reliability
11. Assists other employees without being asked
12. Uses good judgment in resolving ministry problems
13. Requires little direction and supervision
14. Works well in a team

Overall performance comments: The leader should highlight accomplishments, significant achievements, recognized strengths, and areas requiring improvement.

Overall performance level: Include an overall assessment of the team member's performance (E, V, S, NI).

Action plan for further development and training: The leader should identify specific plans for improving performance and any training available to the team member.

QUESTIONS TO PONDER

How does1 Corinthians 12:12–26 inform us about the importance of team ministry?

If you were asked to form a ministry team, what purpose statement would you develop for it?

What position descriptions would you develop for the team?

What training and resourcing would be needed for the team?

RECOMMENDED RESOURCE

The Mentor Leader: Secrets to Building People and Teams That Win Consistently (2011) by Tony Dungy

CONCLUSION

What has preceded this final chapter is, in effect, a leader's ecosystem—a system or a group of interconnected elements, formed by the interaction of a community of organisms with their environment. A leader's ecosystem includes the interaction of the head, heart, and hand—the section titles of this book. The principles and practices, whether head, heart, or hand, in this book inform, influence, and condition each other.

For instance, when a leader determines the hills they will die on, the hills God has called them to bleed on, and the hills they will not climb, the specifics will impact circle-of-concern and circle-of-influence issues—the things you can personally change and those items that you cannot change.

Likewise, making good and wise decisions will be informed by the beliefs and values you hold. The effectiveness in implementing a strategy, procedure, methodology, or tactic will be conditioned by a leader's beliefs and values. Your reading practices and absorption of what matters will inform your practices as a leader.

More specifically, the principles and practices under the Head section will affect the principles and practices discussed under the Heart section. In turn, the practices under the Hand section will be inspired by the matters discussed under Head and Heart. Regardless, you will benefit by engaging any topic in and of itself, irrespective of which section and which topic in that section is addressed.

I encourage you, as a leader, to prioritize your needs now, engage the appropriate topic, and implement them as suggested. For example, if leaders believe that making good decisions is a priority, then they should focus on that topic. If leaders are unclear about their calling, they should attend to the topic of calling. If leaders are responsible for identifying and recruiting people, they might want to concentrate on the topic of recruiting. If developing leaders is a priority, the leader probably should select the topic of developing in the Hand section.

Although the topics presented in this book are not exhaustive, they include what I believe are the essential areas of effective leadership. Also, the references used may seem dated, but I have found these resources most helpful in exercising my leadership. Hopefully, any leader will find something of value that will help them become better leaders.

I encourage you to first scan the topics included in the book, identify those that seem relevant to your situation, prioritize your selections, and begin reading the selected chapters. I also encourage you to implement pertinent and relative practices described in the chapters of immediate interest or utility.

May God richly bless you as you seek to become a better leader.

BIBLIOGRAPHY

Anderson, Leith. *Winning the Values War in a Changing Culture: Thirteen Distinct Values That Mark a Follower of Jesus Christ.* Minneapolis: Bethany House Publishers, 1994.

Anderson, Neil T. *The Bondage Breaker.* Eugene: Harvest House Publishers, 2000.

Blanchard, Ken, Patricia Zigarmi, and Drea Zigarmi. *Leadership and the One Minute Manager: Increasing Effectiveness Through Situational Leadership II.* New York: William Morrow, 2013.

Bolman, Lee G., and Terrence E. Deal. *Reframing Organizations: Artistry, Choice, and Leadership.* Hoboken: Jossey-Bass, 2013.

Bonhoeffer, Dietrich. *The Way to Freedom: Letters, Lectures and Notes from the Collected Works.* Mineola: Fount Publisher, 1972.

Bonhoeffer, Dietrich. "Lectio Divina (Divine Reading)." *Selah Center.* 2016. http://selahcenter.org/lectio-divina/.

Bourgond, Greg. *Papa's Blessings: The Gift That Keeps Giving.* Bloomington: iUniverse Publishing, 2011.

_____. *A Rattling of Sabers: Preparing Your Heart for Life's Battles.* Bloomington: iUniverse Publishing, 2012.

_____. *Setting Your Course: How to Navigate Your Life's Journey.* Bloomington: iUniverse Publishing, 2014.

Clinton, J. Robert. *Reading on the Run: Continuum Reading Concepts, Leadership Series.* Altadena: Barnabas Publishers, 1987.

_____. *Leadership Emergence Theory: A Self-Study Manual for Analyzing the Development of a Christian Leader.* Altadena: Barnabas Publishers, 1989.

_____. *Handbook I: Leaders, Leadership and the Bible: An Overview, the Bible and Leadership Series.* Altadena: Barnabas Publishers, 1993.

_____. "Finishing Well—Six Characteristics." *ScribD*, 2007. Accessed November 27, 2017. https://www.scribd.com/document/108953 759/Finishing Well-Six Characteristics.

_____. *The Making of a Leader: Recognizing the Lessons and Stages of Leadership Development*. Colorado Springs: NavPress, 2012.

Clinton, Richard, and Paul Leavenworth. *Finishing Well: Establishing a Lasting Legacy*, vol. 3. Amazon.com: CreateSpace Independent Publishing Platform, 2012.

_____. *Starting Well: Building a Strong Foundation for a Lifetime of Ministry*. Altadena: Barnabas Publishers, 2012.

Cordeiro, Wayne. *Doing Church as a Team*. Ventura: Regal Books, 2001.

Covey, Stephen R. *First Things First*. New York: Free Press, 1996.

_____. *The 7 Habits of Highly Effective People*. New York: Free Press, 2004.

Dickman, Chris. "Creative Thinking Methods and Techniques." *StockLogos*, 2014. Accessed November 27, 2017. http: members. ozemail.com.au/-caveman/Creative/Techniques/.

Dungy, Tony, Jim Caldwell, and Nathan Whitaker. *The Mentor Leader: Secrets to Building People and Teams That Win Consistently*. Carol Stream: Tyndale Momentum, 2011.

Fields, Linda. *IMPACT Your Sphere of INFLUENCE: Bringing God's Presence in the Workplace*. Fields Enterprise Solutions, 2013.

Finley, James. *Christian Meditation: Experiencing the Presence of God*. San Francisco: HarperOne, 2005.

Ford, Leighton. *Transforming Leadership: Jesus' Way of Creating Vision, Shaping Values & Empowering Change*. Downers Grove: InterVarsity Press, 1993.

Foster, Richard J. *Celebration of Discipline: The Path to Spiritual Growth*. San Francisco: Harper, 2002.

Friesen, Garry, and J. Robin Maxson. *Decision Making and the Will of God*. Colorado Springs: Multnomah Books, 2004.

Harris, Brian. "Conducting a Spiritual Audit: A First Fifteen of Questions ..." *Brian Harris*. October 20, 2015.

Accessed October 20, 2017. http://brianharrisauthor.com/conducting-a-spiritual-audit-a-first-fifteen-of-questions/.

Hart, Archibald D. *Adrenaline & Stress: The Exciting New Breakthrough That Helps You Overcome Stress Damage.* Waco: Word Books, 1986.

———. "Adrenalin-Fed Spirituality." *Preaching Today.* June 1998. http://www.preachingtoday.com/illustrations1998/june/4430.html.

Hersey, Paul. *The Situational Leader.* Escondido: Center for Leadership Studies, 1997.

Hersey, Paul, Kenneth H. Blanchard, and Dewey E. Johnson. *Management of Organizational Behavior.* London: Pearson Education, 2012.

Kogan, Kory, Suzette Blakemore, and James Wood. *Project Management for the Unofficial Project Manager: A Franklin Covey Title.* Dallas: BenBella Books, 2015.

Krejcir, Richard J. "10 Ways to Improve Relational Skills." *Into the Word.* 1980. Accessed November 27, 2017. www.intothyword.org/apps/articles/default.asp? articleid'32152.

Lawrence, Rick. *The Jesus-Centered Life: The Life You Didn't Think Possible, With the Jesus You Never Knew.* Loveland: Group Publishing, 2016.

Lawrenz, Mel, and Skye Jethani. *Spiritual Influence: The Hidden Power Behind Leadership.* Grand Rapids: Zondervan, 2012.

Leas, Speed B. *Discover Your Conflict Management Style.* Lanham: Rowman & Littlefield Publishers, 1998.

Lewis, G. Douglas. *Resolving Church Conflicts: A Case Study Approach for Local Congregations.* New York: HarperCollins Publishers, 1981.

Lindgren, Alvin J., and Norman Shawchuck. *Management for Your Church: How to Realize Your Church's Potential through a Systems Approach.* Nashville: Organization Resources Press, 1984.

MacArthur, John, Nathan Busenitz, Scott Lang, Phil Johnson, Daniel Gillespie, Rick Hollan, Carey Hardy, Kurt Gebhards, and Dan Dumas. *Fool's Gold? Discerning Truth in an Age of Error.* Edited by John MacArthur. Wheaton: Crossway Books, 2005.

MacArthur, John. *The Power of Integrity: Building a Life Without Compromise.* Wheaton: Crossway Publishing, 1997.

Malphurs, Aubrey. *Building Leaders: Blueprints for Developing Leadership at Every Level of Your Church.* Grand Rapids: Baker Books, 2004.

_____. *Advanced Strategic Planning: A 21st-Century Model for Church and Ministry Leaders.* Grand Rapids: Baker Books, 2013.

Maxwell, John C. *Developing the Leaders Around You.* Nashville: Nelson Business, 2005.

_____. *The Maxwell Daily Reader: 365 Days of Insight to Develop the Leader Within You and Influence Those Around You.* Nashville: Thomas Nelson, 2007.

Olson, David T. *Discovering Your Leadership Style: The Power of Chemistry, Strategy and Spirituality.* Downers Grove: InterVarsity Press, 2014.

Packer, J. I. *Knowing God.* Downers Grove: InterVarsity Press, 1973.

Patterson, Ben. *Serving God: The Grand Essentials of Work and Worship.* Downers Grove: InterVarsity Press, 1994.

Polya, George. "How to Solve It: A New Aspect of Mathematical Method." 1973. Accessed November 27, 2017. https: notendur. hi.is/hei2/teaching/Polya _HowtoSolveIt.pdf.

Rush, Myron, and Myron D. Rush. *Management: A Biblical Approach.* Colorado Springs: David C. Cook, 2002.

Sande, Ken. *The Peacemaker: A Biblical Guide to Resolving Personal Conflict.* Ada: Baker Books, 2004.

Sheveland, Jerry, and Greg Bourgond. *Empowering Leaders for a Disciple-Making Church.* College Avenue Baptist Church: San Diego, 1992.

Sibley, Bryan M.D. *God First: Setting Life's Priorities.* Lafayette: Acadian House Publishing, 2016.

Smith, Fred. "Conducting A Spiritual Audit: 12 Questions to Keep Your Personal Accounts in Order." *Leadership* (winter 1998). www. thelifethatlistens.com/other/Conducting_a_Spiritual_Audit.doc.

Stanley, Paul D., and J. Robert Clinton. *Connecting: The Mentoring Relationships You Need to Succeed in Life.* Colorado Springs: NavPress, 1992.

Swenson Richard A., MD. *Margin: Restoring Emotional, Physical, Financial, and Time Reserves to Overloaded Lives.* Colorado Springs: NavPress, 1992.

Tuhovsky, Ian, and Wendell Wadsworth. *Communication Skills: A Practical Guide to Improving Your Social Intelligence, Presentation, Persuasion and Public Speaking.* Edited by Wendell Wadsworth. Amazon.com: CreateSpace Independent Publishing Platform, 2015.

Walling, Terry B. *Stuck!: Navigating the Transitions of Life & Leadership.* Amazon.com: CreateSpace Independent Publishing Platform, 2015.

Webb, Keith E., and Gary R. Collins. *The COACH Model for Christian Leaders: Powerful Leadership Skills for Solving Problems, Reaching Goals, and Developing Others.* Google Books, 2012.

Wenger, Win. "CPS Techniques." *Project Renaissance.* 2015. Accessed November 27, 2017. http://www.winwenger.com/mind.htm.

Willard, Dallas. *Renovation of the Heart: Putting on the Character of Christ.* Colorado Springs: NavPress, 2012.

Williams, Dave. *Emerging Leaders: A New Breed of Church Leadership for the 21st Century.* Lansing: Decapolis Publishing, 2010.

Yeung, Rob. *Successful Interviewing and Recruitment: Structure the Interview; Identify Exceptional Candidates; Hire the Best Person for the Job.* London: Kogan Page, 2010.

Youngblood, Ronald F., F. F. Bruce, R. K. Harrison. *Nelson's Illustrated Bible Dictionary: New and Enhanced Edition.* Nashville: Thomas Nelson Publishers, 2014.

ABOUT THE AUTHOR

Gregory W. Bourgond, DMin, EdD

President and Founder

Heart of a Warrior Ministries
Shoreview, Minnesota
Website: www.heartofawarrior.org
Email: HOAWAdvance@aol.com
Phone: 651-308-1530
Learner / Activator /Achiever / Input / Belief

Dr. Greg Bourgond earned a bachelor's degree in psychology from Chapman University (1979), a master of divinity degree (MDiv.) from Bethel Seminary in San Diego (1983), a doctor of ministry degree (DMin.) in church leadership from Bethel in Saint Paul (1997), and an EdD in instructional technology and distance education (2001) from Nova Southeastern University. He completed postgraduate studies in the Institute for Educational Management at Harvard Graduate School of Education (2003). He is the author of award-winning books such as *A Rattling of Sabers: Preparing Your Heart for Life's Battles*, published in 2010 and 2012; *Papa's Blessings: The Gift That Keeps Giving*, published in 2011; and *Setting Your Course: How to Navigate Life's Journey*, published in 2014.

His previous experience includes ten years in the defense industry and commercial business and over eighteen years in various ministry positions. He has held positions as a principal analyst and project manager for Analysis & Technology, Inc., senior project engineer for Hughes Aircraft Company, unit training manager for General Electric, and general manager in Burdick Companies. In ministry, he has been a deacon, elder, ministry director, associate pastor, and executive pastor in San Diego and Rochester. He completed twenty-nine years of active and reserve duty in enlisted and officer ranks in the US Navy.

He completed four years as executive pastor of Christ Community Church in Rochester and is currently the director of Online Coaching Certification for Ministry Advantage and president and founder of Heart of Warrior Ministries. He serves in several consulting roles with other ministry organizations. He served as assistant to the provost of Bethel University and director of Strategy for Online Education, providing direction for advancement of online education across Bethel

University's four academic units. He provided operational support to Bethel Seminary in the areas of distributed learning, budget development, and future strategic operations. He has also served as vice president for Operations and Strategic Initiatives, dean for the Center of Transformational Leadership, and dean of Academic Affairs and Instructional Technology at Bethel Seminary.

Greg serves as a consultant and teacher in the areas of leadership formation and development, spiritual and personal formation, legacy, life mapping and focused living, organizational systems theory and applications, operational effectiveness, ministry planning, strategic planning, distance learning and technology-mediated course delivery, men's ministry, small-group dynamics, and mentoring. As president and founder of Heart of a Warrior Ministries, his ministry is dedicated to helping men live lives of integrity and honor under the authority of God. He has taught in graduate and postgraduate schools and ministry organizations and has spoken and preached in many churches and ministry contexts around the world. He has also twice been C. S. Lewis Visiting Scholar-in-Residence at the Kilns in Headington, England. Greg has been happily married for forty-nine years and enjoys his grandchildren every chance he gets.

MY OTHER BOOKS

God is very clear about his purposes for you. If you want to live a meaningful life, it must be aligned with his purposes. You have a unique purpose to fulfill, a committed passion to embrace, a role to perform, unique methodologies—a personal tool kit—to employ, and an ultimate contribution to make. In *Setting Your Course*, you are encouraged set your course, find focus for your life, engage in God's journey for you, and finish your journey well. He employs a three-part process to influence you to live all-out for Christ—the compass, map, and guide. The *compass* explains the importance of orienting your life in accordance with established biblical compass points. The *map* defines the trajectory you are to follow, based on how God has wired you. The *guide* stresses the importance of being mentored and mentoring others. *Setting Your Course* helps you formulate a deliberate strategy for determining your purpose; assists you in aligning your life, according to God's plan; encourages you to become a proactive partner in fulfilling God's purposes and redemptive activity; and exhorts you to leave a worthwhile legacy in the lives of others.

Every human being longs for the affirmation, acceptance, and esteem of someone who matters to them. Sadly, most of us never hear the words we long to hear—words of appreciation, esteem, recognition, and value. In *Papa's Blessings*, the vital importance of bestowing blessings upon others is stressed. This practical and helpful guide provides a fresh take on applying an ancient practice to life in the modern world. The book establishes the importance of blessing, identifies the eight essential components of a meaningful blessing, provides multiple examples of blessings, describes how to administer a blessing, explains the legacy of blessings, and includes a worksheet for developing and giving a blessing. *Papa's Blessings* combines biblical references, illustrations, and personal and emotional stories to show it's never too late or too early to give a blessing to those who long for one, beginning with your loved ones and continuing with those who come within your sphere of influence. The world can be a cold and unforgiving place, and *Papa's Blessings* helps prepare our loved ones by giving them something that will sustain them on the difficult journey before them—a blessing.

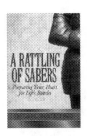

In *A Rattling of Sabers: Preparing Your Heart for Life's Battles,* men are led on a spiritual journey that will help them embrace a renewed relationship with Christ and a life filled with authenticity, integrity, courage, and honor under the authority of God. Dr. Bourgond, founder of Heart of a Warrior Ministries, has dedicated nearly four decades to ministering to men through discipleship, mentoring, teaching, and leadership development. While guiding men on a journey to wholeness by helping them tune their own hearts to the heart of God, Dr. Bourgond shares life illustrations and fresh theological insights that will teach men to become aware of their unique wiring and God's purposes for their lives. Dr. Bourgond identifies situational lifestyles that men adopt to navigate the pathways of our lives, addresses the real battlefield for change and transformation that will help men reach the objectives of God's preferred lifestyle, and provides guidance on how to correct corrupted behavior and proactively live a godly life. *A Rattling of Sabers* offers a unique and inspirational map that allows men to bring glory and honor to God and be encouraged to actively live the life that God has chosen for each of them.

Printed in the United States
by Baker & Taylor Publisher Services